The Cooking
of
Greece

The Cooking
of
Greece

Tony Schmaeling

Ω
OMEGA BOOKS

ACKNOWLEDGEMENTS

Travelling through Greece is a great adventure. Greek food and wine are part of the experience and without it, the picture would be incomplete. Planning a gastronomic tour of the country is not easy and it was thanks to the help received from Mr Josephopoulos and Miss Pollatos of 'Hermes en Grece' and Mrs Greenberg and Miss Paliadow Lia of the Greek Government Tourist Office in Athens that the tour turned out to be a success. I also extend my thanks to all the officers of the Greek Government Tourist Office and the chefs and owners of restaurants who contributed by sharing with me their food and recipes.

In Sydney my friends Venus and Mike Kasamatis corrected my Greek spelling, while Gwen and Michelle Flanders did their best to decipher reams of my illegible longhand and typed it into a neat manuscript.

My editor, Susan Tomnay once more applied her great skill in putting the whole book together.

The original idea of this series of cookbooks on the food of Europe came from Kevin Weldon, at the time Managing Director of Paul Hamlyn. I thank him, Warwick Jacobson, the company's Publishing Manager and Anne Wilson, the Chief Editor for their encouragement and technical support.

I thank Graham Turnbull of Traveland for his company's assistance in my travels through Europe to collect material for this series. His London office gave me valuable assistance.

David Davis, my camera assistant, was a great help and untiring travel companion.

All flour is plain (all-purpose) flour unless otherwise specified

This edition published 1983 by Omega Books Ltd,
1 West Street, Ware, Hertfordshire, under licence
from the proprietor.

ISBN 0 907853 12 9

Printed and bound in Hong Kong by South China Printing Co.

CONTENTS

THRACE

MACEDONIA

Philippi
Kavala
Pella
Thessaloniki
Thassos

Mt. Athos

Platamon
Lemnos

EPIRUS
Corfu
Parga
Meteora
Larissa
THESSALY
Trikala
SPORADES
ISLANDS

Paxi
Skiathos
Alonissos
Lesbos

Kalambaka

EASTERN AEGEAN ISLANDS

Lamia

Ithaca
CENTRAL GREECE
Delphi
Itea
EUBOEA

Levadia
Rafina

Sami
Patras
IONIAN ISLANDS
Corinth
Athens
Andros
AEGEAN ISLANDS

Kefalonia
Olympia
Nafplion
Lavrion
Tinos
Mykonos

Aegina
Poros
Kea
Patmos
Leros

PELOPONNESE
Tripolis
Hydra
Kythnos
Syros
Delos
DODECANESE
ISLANDS

Kalamata
Mystra
Serifos
Kalymnos
Kos

Sifnos
Paros
Naxos
Symi

Sparta
Milos
Ios
Rhodes

Santorini
Lindos

CYCLADES ISLANDS

Karpathos

Chania
Rethymnon
Heraklion

CRETE
Ag. Nikolaos

Ierapetra

The Regions of
GREECE

INTRODUCTION
Where the East Meets the West

The soft light of autumn greeted my arrival on Greek soil as my ship berthed in Corfu town. I was full of anticipation, as it was the beginning of my gastronomic tour of Greece. Having always been keen on Greek food, I was now looking forward to trying it in the original. Corfu, I felt, was a good starting point.

Fish and seafood, of very good quality here on Corfu, is in general one of the main sources of food throughout Greece and its islands. This is quite natural, as the three seas that wash the endless shores bring forth a rich catch. The Mediterranean, the Ionian and Aegean Seas supply the Greek kitchen with a great variety of seafood.

During my travels along the shores of Greece, I would regularly stop to buy freshly caught fish and try to glean interesting recipes from the fishermen, like the Fisherman's Wife's Fish Soup given to me on one sunny morning near the Canal of Corinth (see p. 28).

Greeks like cooking their fish with vegetables and one of the tastiest preparations is Psári Plakí cooked in the oven with tomatoes, spinach, zucchini, onions, celery, potatoes and topped with lemon slices – a meal in itself, especially if eaten with fresh crusty bread and washed down with retsina. To me this combination epitomises the 'true Greek flavour'.

A great deal of Greek cooking is a result of making wholesome and tasty dishes out of modest ingredients. Hearty soups, especially those made with dried beans and lentils, served with salads, fresh bread and wine, are frequently the entire meal. The necessity to make the best of things is also responsible for the many nourishing stews so popular as family meals.

Religious festivities and observances strongly influence eating habits. Easter not only celebrates the Resurrection but also is the breaking of the Lenten fast, strictly observed in Greece; seven weeks when meat, even fish, eggs, butter, milk, cheese and any other animal products are forbidden.

The faithful congregate in the churches just before midnight, then as the clock strikes twelve the lighting of candles symbolises the rising of Christ. At home immediately after the Mass a light supper is the first non-Lenten meal: a meat soup and colourful Easter eggs.

The people celebrate Easter Sunday with a feast of spit-roasted lamb, Easter bread and many other dishes forbidden during Lent, all washed down with lots of retsina.

Hospitality and gregariousness are two great Greek characteristics and they both revolve around eating and drinking. Not only are strangers invited to partake in the Resurrection meal, but in everyday life drink and food are offered to a visitor anytime he may call. It may be just a traditional cup of strong Greek coffee, some sweetmeats and a glass of cold water, but custom demands such a gesture and it is correct for the guest to accept.

The taverna is a great Greek institution. It is the type of bar where people spend hours sipping Ouzo or retsina and picking from a wide variety of Mezéthes, talking and gossiping, solving the problems of the world and playing cards.

In Greece the main meal is eaten during the middle of the day. Shops, offices and institutions close about 1 o'clock and everybody adjourns for lunch. This is then followed by a siesta break of three hours. Everybody returns to work at 5 pm and work continues till 8 or 9 pm. Dinner is eaten late, between 10 and 11 pm, and therefore is usually a light meal. This type of routine is very much the pattern of similar customs along the European shores of the Mediterranean.

Olives, extensively grown throughout Greece are also one of the most important products of the Greek economy. Eaten with every meal of the day and many times in between, they are gathered either unripe and green or well ripened and black and preserved in brine. Famous are the black vinegary olives of Kalamata in the southern Peleponnese and so are the green olives of Itea near Delphi. It would be difficult to imagine the Greek landscape without the twisted black trunks of ancient olive trees and the dull silvery shimmer of their leaves.

Cheese has been eaten since ancient times and none is better known than feta. Made from goats', sheep or cow's milk, it is used daily, its white firm texture and lightly pungent and salty taste is one of the typical flavours of Greece.

Grapes, grown here since ancient times, produce wines of reasonable quality. The universally loved wine in Greece and well known elsewhere is retsina which originated in ancient times when wines were kept in goat skins lined with pine resin to preserve and seal them. The taste became popular and now the flavour is added to satisfy the demand. Best drunk chilled, it is a perfect match with the strong flavour of Greek food.

A gathering of Greeks in a taverna would be hard to imagine without Ouzo, the anise-flavoured spirit which turns cloudy when water is added.

You only have to look around and count the innumerable pastry shops to realise that the Greeks have a very sweet tooth. A cup of coffee is seldom drunk without something sweet to eat with it. While a meal usually finishes with fresh fruit, a Greek will not forego dessert which usually follows an hour or two after the meal. The Baklavá – that luscious sweet made with layers of filo pastry, nuts, spices and drenched in a syrup of sugar, honey and lemon juice – is the best known Greek dessert, but there are other sweet things: cream puffs, custard cream, fruit tarts, cakes glistening with chocolate cream, glazed fruit, nut-studded biscuits, the very Middle Eastern halva, and Loukoumia, universally known as Turkish Delight.

Greece, perforce of time and circumstance, has despite its Western ways in many respects remained a country orientated towards the East, and a culinary visit to Greece can be taken as an introduction to the food of the Middle East.

FIRST COURSES AND HORS D'OEUVRES

Greeks are gregarious people and what better way of getting together with friends than after a day's work, at the local taverna over a glass of wine or Ouzo. But drinking without eating would be quite unthinkable, so a great Greek tradition of eating Mezéthes has developed.

In their simplest form they may be just bowls of local olives and small pieces of feta cheese. Their range is huge: Dolmádes (rice-stuffed vine leaves), cheese and spinach wrapped in filo pastry, Taramosaláta, pieces of roasted meat, pieces of seafood marinated in a lemony dressing, nuts and seeds, dried fruit, eggplant dips – a never-ending list.

During the warm summer evenings this traditional Greek 'cocktail hour' is enjoyed in the open. Chairs and tables are set on the footpaths or terraces in front of the taverna. Everybody is there to observe and to be observed. Greeks like talking a lot and so the art of conversation is given free rein. Like the Mezéthes, there is no limit to the topic for discussion, and even the most weighty problems of the world are finally resolved!

Some of the dishes, especially the more substantial ones, can form part of the dinner at home and are served as a first course.

Simple or complicated, most of them have one characteristic in common: they are piquant in one way or another and, of course, their main aim is to stimulate the appetite. Who could fail to have the taste buds excited after a few mouthfuls of Tzatziki, the slightly acid and clean-tasting combination of yogurt and fresh crisp cucumber? And what about Sikotákia, lamb's livers with lemon juice? Or the tart eggplant dip.

Washed down with glasses of retsina or Ouzo, the Mezéthes are a great beginning to any meal.

Taverna Costoyanis, Athens

Costoyanis is situated just behind the National Archaeological Museum, and judging by the evening's crowd is just as popular.

Unpretentiously the guests enter through part of the kitchen where, before they go to their tables, they can feast their eyes on enormous displays of Greek specialities. They are encouraged to talk to the chef and consult him on what is best on the night's menu. There are many fish and seafood dishes; and if the number of Japanese guests is any indication, they must be good.

During my evening there I tried many of the dishes. Some were conventional and traditional: stuffed tomatoes and peppers, Moussaká and different eggplant dishes. Standard to most Greek restaurants, at Costoyanis they were particularly good.

Others, like the stuffed squid, were exquisite and I now know why the Imam swooned when he had the stuffed eggplant – it must have come from here. The stuffed pheasant, filled with chestnuts and served with a bacon and mushroom sauce, was exceptionally good.

The restaurant was buzzing with spirited conversation. At one stage people were waiting outside for others to leave, which they were obviously reluctant to do.

Right: Clockwise from bottom left: Baked Lamb and Tomato in Béchamel Sauce; Stuffed Squid (p. 74); Fish Mayonnaise Salad; Lamb Fricassée with Avgolemono Sauce (p. 90); Braised Eggplant with onion and tomato (p. 49); Stuffed Tomato and Pepper.

Dolmadakia

Rice-stuffed Vine Leaves

*Preserved vine leaves are commercially available from delicatessen shops. However, fresh young vine leaves can be easily prepared for use in this recipe. It was given to me by the **Restaurant Kuyu** in Piraeus.*

Preparation of vine leaves:

If fresh vine leaves are used immediately, rinse them in cold water, then blanch them in boiling water for 3 minutes, drain, allow to cool and use as described in the recipe.

To preserve, select clean leaves, not larger than 15 cm (6 in). Wash them in cold water. Cut off the stems and place them in stacks of 15-20 leaves with the dull side facing up. Roll them tightly and tie them with a string. Boil 2 litres (8 cups) of water, add 125 g (4 oz) salt, and place the rolled-up leaves into the water. Boil for 3 minutes. Remove the bundles, cool them slightly and arrange them in 2-3 cup jars. Pour the boiling salt water into the jars, filling them to the top and seal them tightly. The leaves preserved in this fashion do not require refrigeration.

Preparation of the Dolmadakia:

Yields 36

⅔ cup (5 fl oz) olive oil
3 large onions, finely chopped
6 spring onions (scallions), finely chopped
1 teaspoon salt
freshly ground black pepper
2 tablespoons pine nuts
150 g (¾ cup) rice
1 tablespoon finely chopped dill

½ bunch parsley, finely chopped
1 teaspoon finely chopped mint
juice ½ lemon
1 cup (8 fl oz) water
36 vine leaves
parsley stalks
lemon wedges
parsley sprigs

1. In half of the olive oil, sauté the onions and spring onions until they are soft and transparent.
2. Add the salt, pepper, pine nuts and rice. Cook for 10 minutes, stirring from time to time.
3. Add the dill, parsley, mint, lemon juice and the water, cover the saucepan and simmer for approximately 10 minutes, until the water is absorbed. Season if necessary.
4. Spread the vine leaves with the dull side up and on each place a teaspoonful of stuffing. First fold the stalk end of the leaf over the stuffing, then the right-hand side, followed by the left-hand side. Finally, starting with the stalk-end roll the vine leaf firmly into a cylindrical shape. Squeeze it gently in the palm of your hand to keep it intact.
5. Place the parsley stalks on the bottom of the saucepan and arrange the stuffed vine leaves in layers on top of them. Weight them down with an inverted plate.

6. Combine the remaining olive oil, 2 tablespoons of lemon juice and enough water to barely cover the plate.
7. Cover the saucepan, bring slowly to the boil and gently simmer for 1½ hours.
8. Remove from the stove and permit the Dolmadakia to cool for 2 to 3 hours or overnight.
9. To serve, arrange them on a serving platter and present them at room temperature or slightly chilled and garnished with lemon wedges and parsley sprigs.

Taramosaláta

Fish Roe Spread
From **Restaurant Kuyu,** *Piraeus*

Taramosaláta is a spread used on canapés or as a dip with raw vegetables, and is one of the most popular of all Greek hors d'oeuvres. Taramá is the salted roe of the grey mullet, tuna fish or smoked cod. It is readily obtainable from Continental delicatessen shops. The recipe described here is from one of the many seafood restaurants that are along the quay of the Mikrolimano of Piraeus. Other recipes use potatoes instead of bread, beaten egg yolks and no onions at all. I recommend that having tried this basic recipe, the reader experiments with other combinations.

Yields 1 ½ cups

125 g (4 oz) Taramá (salted roe of the grey mullet or tuna or smoked roe of cod)
4 slices stale white bread without crust

juice 1½-2 lemons
1 small onion, finely grated
1 garlic clove, crushed
1 cup (8 fl oz) olive oil

1. Taste the roe and if too salty, soak it for 5 to 10 minutes. Drain.
2. Soak the bread in some water for a few minutes and squeeze dry.
3. Combine all ingredients, except the oil, in a food processor and mix until they are creamy, then gradually add the oil. A blender can also be used. If making the Taramosaláta by hand, mash the ingredients with a fork or a potato masher; finally, using a whisk, mix in the olive oil. Serve chilled.

Oktapodi Toursi

Octopus Salad
From **Restaurant Kuyu**, *Piraeus*

Octopus abounds in the warm waters along the Greek shores. It is prepared in many ways and is particularly popular when simply marinated in vinegar or lemon and served as an appetiser. Medium-sized octopus, of not more than 1 kg (2 lb) in weight, is preferable. The fish merchants sell it already tenderised and the cleaning and preparation is relatively simple. Vinegar or lemon juice is used in the marinade. I personally prefer lemon juice which complements the sea flavour of octopus.

Serves 6

1 kg (2 lb) octopus
½ clove garlic, finely chopped
1 small onion finely chopped
½ cup (4 fl oz) olive oil
juice 2-3 lemons, or ½ cup
  (4 fl oz) white wine vinegar or
  cider vinegar

salt
freshly ground black pepper
lemon wedges and parsley sprigs
  for garnish

1. Clean the octopus in the sink under running water. Cut off the tentacles.
2. On a low heat simmer the tentacles and other fleshy parts in a saucepan for about 1 hour. Usually there should be enough of its own juice, but if necessary add a little water if the juices have evaporated.
3. Taste, and when tender remove from heat. When cool cut it into small pieces.
4. In a bowl or jar combine all the ingredients (having selected either lemon juice or vinegar for the marinade). Season to taste.
5. Cover and marinate for at least 12 hours, turning the pieces occasionally.
6. Serve in a dish garnished with lemon wedges and parsley sprigs.

Right: Yacht haven and fishing harbour of Mikrolimano, Piraeus.

Tiropites

Cheese Triangle Puffs
*From **Amalia Hotel**, Olympia*

In Greece these tasty crisp 'pasties' are served not only as savouries at cocktail parties but also for dinner as small appetisers or as a main course. Using filo pastry which is readily available in delicatessen shops, they are easily and quickly prepared. While preparing them double the quantity and deep freeze half for future use when they only have to be reheated to be ready for an unexpected guest.

Depending on their size this recipe will yield between 36 and 48 puffs.

250 g (8 oz) feta cheese, finely crumbled
185 g (6 oz) Gruyère or mature Cheddar-style cheese, grated
3 eggs, lightly beaten
4 sprigs parsley, finely chopped

freshly ground black pepper
salt
250 g (8 oz) filo pastry sheets
100 g (3½ oz) melted butter

1. Preheat the oven to 200°C (400° F/Gas 6).
2. Combine the feta, the Gruyère or Cheddar, the eggs, parsley and pepper. Taste before adding the salt, as the mixture may be sufficiently seasoned. Mix thoroughly until all ingredients are well blended.
3. Cut the leaves of the filo pastry lengthways into three equal strips. Cover them with a damp teatowel so that the sheets do not dry out. One strip will be required per puff.
4. Lay out one strip and brush it with melted butter. Fold it in half, brush it again with butter.
5. Place a teaspoon of the mixture on the end of the strip.
6. Fold corner of pastry over the filling and continue folding as illustrated.
7. Place the triangles on a buttered baking tin, brush tops with melted butter and bake in the preheated oven for 12 to 15 minutes until they are plump, crisp and golden. Serve hot.

Avgá Saláta

Egg Salad
Serves 6-8

12 hard-boiled eggs, chopped
1 cup (8 fl oz) mayonnaise (see p. 141)
1 small onion, grated
1 clove garlic, crushed juice 1 lemon

4 sprigs dill, finely chopped
1 sprig fresh thyme (or ½ teaspoon dried thyme)
freshly ground black pepper
salt

1. Combine all ingredients, refrigerate.
2. Serve either as salad or appetiser.

Tzatziki

Cucumber Yogurt Dip
Yields 2 ½ cups (20 fl oz)

2 cucumbers, peeled and seeds removed
salt
¾ cup (6 fl oz) plain yogurt
½ cup (4 fl oz) sour cream

½ clove garlic, crushed
juice ½ lemon
⅛ teaspoon cayenne pepper

1. Cut the cucumber into pieces 2.5-5 cm (1-2 in) long and purée in a food processor or blender.
2. Place the purée in a colander, sprinkle with salt and let it stand to drain for 20 minutes.
3. Combine the remaining ingredients, add the cucumber purée and, if necessary, adjust seasoning.
4. Refrigerate for 6 hours and serve as a dip.

Spanakópites

Spinach Cheese Puffs
Except for the different stuffing, these puffs are prepared exactly as the Tiropites (cheese triangle puffs), (see p. 16).

Filling:
½ cup (4 fl oz) olive oil
6 spring onions (scallions), chopped
1 kg (2 lb) fresh spinach, washed, drained and finely chopped (or 500 g (1 lb) frozen chopped spinach, defrosted)
500 g (1 lb) feta cheese, finely crumbled

300 g (9½ oz) cream cheese
3 sprigs parsley, finely chopped
freshly ground black pepper
1 teaspoon chopped dill
6 eggs, well beaten
500 g (1 lb) filo pastry
220 g (7 oz) melted butter

1. In the oil, lightly fry the spring onions. Add the spinach and sauté until moisture evaporates.
2. In a bowl, combine the feta, cream cheese, parsley, pepper, dill and eggs. Add the spinach and onions. Mix well.
3. Proceed from step 3 of method for the preparation of Tiropetes (Cheese triangle puffs) on p. 16.
   Instead of making the puffs into triangles, they may be formed into little rolls, by placing a teaspoon of the mixture on the end of the buttered strip and rolling it.

Kolokithópitta

Zucchini Pie
Makes 12 servings

1.5 kg (3 lb) zucchini
  (courgettes), unpeeled, grated
2 onions, finely chopped
2 tablespoons olive oil
4 sprigs dill, chopped
4 sprigs parsley, chopped
3 eggs, beaten

½ teaspoon grated nutmeg
freshly ground black pepper
salt
500 g (1 lb) feta cheese, cut into
  1.5 cm (½ in) cubes
½ cup (4 oz) melted butter
12 sheets filo pastry

1. Preheat the oven to 180°C (350° F/Gas 4).
2. Over low heat, sauté the zucchini and onions in the oil for about 30 to 40 minutes until the moisture evaporates. Stir occasionally.
3. Cool, and in a large bowl combine all ingredients except filo pastry and melted butter.
4. With a little of the melted butter, grease a baking dish, approximately 30 x 25 x 7 cm (12 x 10 x 3 in) in size.
5. On the bottom and up the sides of the dish, place 6 sheets of filo pastry, each sheet generously brushed with melted butter before the next is placed.
6. Spoon the zucchini mixture into the pan and fold the edges of the filo over the mixture.
7. Cover the mixture with the remaining 6 sheets of filo pastry, each in turn well brushed with melted butter. Brush the top with melted butter.
8. Tuck the edges of the covering filo leaves around the inside edges of the pan.
9. Bake in the preheated oven for 45 minutes until golden and crisp. Cool for a few minutes. To serve, cut into squares.

Right: Street scene in the main township of the Monastic State of Mt Athos which for the past thousand years has been run by Greek Orthodox monks. The peninsula has a large number of monasteries, some dating back to the 9th Century which house some of the most valuable artifacts and manuscripts of the Orthodox Church. Access to the Peninsula is strictly controlled and special permits are required. No women are permitted to land on the Peninsula. The last woman ever to set foot there was Empress Theodora some 1100 years ago.

Spanakópitta

Spinach Pie
Makes 20 pieces in a 35 x 25 x 5 cm (14 x 10 x 2 in) baking dish

¼ cup (2 fl oz) olive oil
2 onions, finely chopped
3 spring onions (scallions), chopped
1.75 kg (3½ lb) fresh spinach, washed, drained and finely chopped
3 sprigs dill, finely chopped

3 sprigs parsley, finely chopped
½ teaspoon salt
freshly ground black pepper
375 g (12 oz) feta cheese, finely crumbled
4 eggs, lightly beaten
½ cup (4 oz) melted butter
14 sheets filo pastry

1. Preheat the oven to 180°C (350° F/Gas 4).
2. In a large saucepan, heat the oil and sauté the onions and spring onions until transparent and soft.
3. Add the spinach, cover the pan and cook for 5 minutes.
4. Add dill, parsley, salt and pepper and, while stirring, cook for 10 minutes.
5. Cool. Then add the cheese and mix in the eggs. If necessary, adjust seasoning.
6. With some of the melted butter, brush the baking dish.
7. On the bottom and up the sides of the dish, place 6 sheets of filo pastry, each sheet generously brushed with melted butter before the next is placed.
8. Spoon the spinach mixture into this, smooth the top, and fold the edges of the filo over the mixture.
9. Cover the mixture with the remaining 8 sheets of filo pastry, each in turn, as well as the top, well brushed with the melted butter.
10. Tuck the edges of the covering filo around the inside edges of the pan.
11. Bake in the preheated oven for 45 minutes until golden and crisp. Cool for a few minutes, and serve cut into squares.

Kasséri Tiganitó

Fried Cheese Cubes
A simple yet appetising cocktail snack.

250 g (8 oz) Kasséri or Kefalotíri cheese (if not available, use Gruyère or Parmesan cheese), cut into 2.5 cm (1 in) cubes
2 eggs, lightly beaten

125 g (4 oz) dry breadcrumbs
½ cup (4 fl oz) frying oil
juice 1 lemon
freshly ground black pepper

1. Dip the cheese cubes in the egg and then in the breadcrumbs.
2. Fry them in hot oil and serve on cocktail sticks, sprinkled with lemon juice and freshly ground black pepper.

Sikotákia

Lamb's Liver with Lemon Juice
A delicious appetiser in which the lamb's liver may be substituted with calf's or even chicken liver.

Serves 6

250 g (8 oz) lamb's, calf's or chicken liver cut into 2.5 cm (1 in) cubes

45 g (1½ oz) butter

juice 1 lemon

salt

freshly ground black pepper

3 sprigs fresh oregano, chopped (or 1 teaspoon dried oregano)

1. Fry the liver in hot butter.
2. Sprinkle with lemon juice, salt, pepper and oregano.
3. Serve on cocktail sticks or as a first course garnished with lemon wedges.

Angináres Polita

Artichoke Hearts and Vegetables
The original recipe is for artichoke hearts. However, if young tender artichokes are available, they can be used whole. Prepare the artichokes in accordance with instructions given in recipe for Angináres me Avgolémono on p. 57.
If using the hearts, remove all the leaves from the artichoke.

Serves 6

2 carrots, thinly sliced

4 onions, coarsely chopped

12 small new potatoes, peeled

salt

freshly ground black pepper

3 sprigs fresh dill, chopped

½ cup (4 fl oz) olive oil

juice 2 lemons

2 tablespoons flour

12 small artichokes or artichoke bottoms prepared and cooked as in the recipe on p. 57.

1. Simmer the carrots, onions, potatoes, salt, pepper and dill in water for 15 minutes or until potatoes are soft.
2. Combine the oil, lemon juice and flour and, while stirring, add to the vegetables.
3. Cook for 5 minutes, add the artichokes (or artichoke hearts) and simmer for a further 5 minutes.
4. If necessary, adjust seasoning. Serve cool or chilled.

21

Melitzána Purée

Eggplant Purée
This dish can be served as a first course garnished with olives, lemon wedges, lettuce and tomatoes, or as an hors d'oeuvre dip with crackers.

Serves 6-8

1 kg (2 lb) eggplant (aubergine)
½ cup (2 oz) dry breadcrumbs
1 onion, grated
1 clove garlic, crushed
2 sprigs parsley, finely chopped
salt

freshly ground black pepper
juice 1-2 lemons
½ teaspoon oregano
6 mint leaves, chopped
¾ cup (6 fl oz) olive oil

1. Preheat the oven to 200° C (400° F/Gas 6).
2. Bake the whole unpeeled eggplant for 40 to 60 minutes, until soft.
3. Remove the skin and roughly chop the flesh.
4. If a food processor or blender is available, roughly mix all ingredients (except the oil) together and process 2 cupfuls at a time until puréed.
5. Then gradually add the oil, check seasoning and serve chilled.

Melitzanosalata

Eggplant Dip

3-4 large eggplants (aubergines)
1 clove garlic, crushed
  (or ½ onion finely chopped)

juice ½-1 lemon (depending
  on taste)
½ cup (4 fl oz) olive oil
salt

1. Preheat the oven to 200° C (400° F/Gas 6).
2. Bake the eggplants for 30 to 40 minutes.
3. Cool, and peel.
4. On a cutting board, chop the eggplant flesh very finely. Put it in a mixing bowl.
5. Add the garlic or onion, and the lemon juice, stir with a wooden spoon, and gradually add the oil (as in preparing mayonnaise).
6. Season, and refrigerate. Serve it as a dip with chunky fresh bread.

22

Right : Village street, Lakones, Corfu.

Fétta Soufflé me Hirino

Feta Cheese Soufflé with Ham
Serves 4-6

75 g (2½ oz) butter
4 tablespoons flour
1 cup (8 fl oz) hot milk
⅛ teaspoon white pepper
4 egg yolks, well beaten
¾ cup (3 oz) grated feta cheese

1 tablespoon chopped chives
¾ cup (6 oz) finely chopped ham
6 egg whites, stiffly beaten
salt
2 tablespoons grated Kefalotíri or Parmesan cheese

1. Preheat the oven to 180°C (350° F/Gas 4).
2. Melt 60 g (2 oz) of the butter, add the flour, mix well, and cook for 5 minutes stirring constantly.
3. Add the hot milk, over low heat, whisk to a smooth sauce and cook for 5 minutes.
4. Remove from heat and mix in white pepper, egg yolk, feta cheese, chives and ham. Season to taste.
5. Gently fold in the egg whites.
6. Spoon the mixture into a soufflé dish which has been buttered and sprinkled with 1 tablespoon of the grated cheese.
7. Put it in the preheated oven and bake for 35 minutes.
8. Ten minutes before the soufflé is cooked, sprinkle the top with the rest of the grated cheese.
9. Serve the soufflé immediately it is done, with a bowl of Greek salad.

Kolokithákia Tiganitá

Fried Zucchini
Serves 4

1 cup (4 oz) flour
salt
water

8 small zucchini (courgettes), cut into slices
1 cup (8 fl oz) olive oil
freshly ground black pepper

1. Put ½ cup of the flour in a bowl, add salt and enough water to make a thin batter. Leave it in the refrigerator to rest for 1 hour.
2. Dry the zucchini slices in paper towelling.
3. Dust them thoroughly with the remaining flour. Dip them in the batter and fry them in the preheated oil until they are crisp and golden brown on both sides.
4. Drain them on paper towels, if desired sprinkle them with salt and pepper, and serve hot.

Saganáki

Fried Cheese

A popular snack which, if Kasseri or Kefalotíri cheese are not available, may be made with Parmesan, Romano or sharp Cheddar.

Serves 4

250 g (8 oz) cheese, cut into
   slices 1 cm (½ in) thick
½ cup (2 oz) flour
½ cup (4 fl oz) olive oil

juice 1 lemon
3 sprigs fresh oregano, chopped
   (or 1 tablespoon dried oregano)

1. Dust the cheese slices with flour and fry them in the preheated oil for about ½ minute on each side.
2. Serve hot sprinkled with lemon juice and oregano, with fresh crusty bread, a Greek salad and chilled white wine.

Yigandes Plakí

Baked Beans
Serves 6

500 g (1 lb) dried beans
½ cup (4 fl oz) olive oil
2 onions, finely chopped
1 clove garlic, crushed
3 sprigs parsley, chopped

500 g (1 lb) tomatoes, peeled and
   chopped
2 tablespoons tomato purée
2 sprigs oregano, chopped
salt
freshly ground black pepper

1. Soak the beans in water overnight, or boil the beans in water for 2 minutes and let them soak for 1 hour.
2. Boil the soaked beans for 30 minutes.
3. Preheat the oven to 180°C (350°F/Gas 4).
4. Heat the oil in a saucepan and sauté the onions and garlic until onions are soft and transparent.
5. Add parsley, tomatoes, tomato purée, oregano and seasonings. Cook over medium heat for 10 minutes.
6. Place the beans in a casserole, pour the mixture over them. If too thick, add a little water.
7. Bake, uncovered, in the preheated oven for 30 to 45 minutes. Serve warm directly from the casserole.

SOUPS

Soups do not form a very prominent part of the Greek cooking repertoire. They are eaten mainly in the country and are solid, nourishing thick soups which, eaten with chunky fresh bread, can be a meal in themselves. Beans, lentils, potatoes, rice and vegetables are the main ingredients. Lamb and beef bones and left-overs are cooked up to form the basic stocks.

Along the long coast of the mainland and on the islands different fish soups are prepared from the day's catch. They are among the best I have tasted – and no wonder: the seas that lap the shores of Greece abound with some of the best seafood caught anywhere.

Among the few typically Greek soups, two are very characteristic of that country: Soúpa Avgolémono, the light and tasty chicken stock base flavoured and thickened with lemon and eggs and served with boiled rice. The other, so refreshing for a summer meal, is Tzatziki soup, a crisp and healthy combination of yogurt, cucumbers, lemon juice and garlic.

Metaftsis Restaurant, Volos

Volos is set against the picturesque silhouette of Mt Pilion, the mountain of the legendary Centaurs. Here, in far distant time, these mystical creatures, half-horse, half-men frolicked through the countryside. It is also from Volos that the Argonauts set off in their search for the Golden Fleece.

Modern Volos is a busy commercial seaport and from here ferries leave for the beautiful Sporades Islands.

The fishing harbour is a busy spot. Day in day out, scores of fishing boats tie up at the quay and fresh fish is available every day of the year. It is therefore not surprising to find many restaurants which serve delicious fish specialities.

At the Metaftsis Restaurant – along the waterfront promenade right opposite the entrance to the port facilities and overlooking an attractive bronze monument of the Argonauts' ship – the main attractions are the fish dishes: Psári Lemonato sto Fourno (fish steaks cooked in oil with tomato slices), and Psári Ladorigano (a beautifully scented fish dish with lots of oregano, a popular herb in Greek cooking), and many others.

The attractive Greek custom of inspecting the dishes and deciding upon one's order in the kitchen is strictly observed at the Metaftsis. Everybody flocks into the kitchen to see the fine display of the dishes and to question the chef on the relative merits of the wide selection. For us it was a tasting of all the dishes.

However, Kollios, a whole fish prepared in a similar way to fish Ladorigano but without garlic, was the best. Its freshness and delicate flavour were unmistakable.

Right: Foreground: Baked fish with lemon and tomatoes (p. 68); Centre: Fish with tomatoes, wine and oregano (p. 66); Rear: Whole baked mackerel.

Kakavia I

Fisherman's Wife's Fish Soup

On the road winding its way along the shore from the Canal of Corinth to Athens, I stopped to buy some fish from a fisherman whose boat was tied up at a beach. With the help of a woman who was also there to buy fish and who spoke a little English, the fisherman gave me his wife's favourite recipe.

Serves 8-10

2 onions, roughly chopped
2 carrots, sliced
4 stalks celery, sliced
2 potatoes, diced
4 sprigs parsley, chopped
2 cloves garlic, crushed
½ cup (4 fl oz) oil
4 tomatoes, peeled and roughly chopped
12 cups (3 litres) water

1 cup (8 fl oz) dry white wine
salt
12 black peppercorns
4 bay leaves
1 teaspoon oregano
1.5 kg (3 lb) fish, a selection of 3 or 4 types of fish available on the day
juice 1-2 lemons

1. In a large saucepan fry the onions, carrots, celery, potatoes, parsley and garlic in the oil, until light brown.
2. Add the tomatoes, water, wine, a little salt, peppercorns, bay leaves and oregano. Cover and simmer for 30 minutes.
3. Add the fish. Cover and simmer for 20 minutes.
4. Cool sufficiently so that you can handle the fish. Carefully remove it from the saucepan and remove the flesh from the bones.
5. Discard the bones and return the pieces of fish to the pan.
6. Heat it without boiling, if necessary adjust the seasoning, and serve hot sprinkled with lemon juice, with chunky fresh bread.

Tzatziki Soúpa

Cucumber Yogurt Soup
A healthy, refreshing summer soup.

Serves 6

2 cucumbers, peeled and seeded
4 cups (1 litre) plain yogurt
juice 1 lemon
freshly ground black pepper
6 mint leaves, chopped

1 tablespoon chopped chives
½ clove garlic, crushed
½ teaspoon sugar
salt
3 sprigs parsley, for garnish

1. Grate or finely chop the cucumber.
2. Combine all ingredients, except parsley. Season.
3. Refrigerate 1-2 hours and serve in chilled bowls sprinkled with parsley.
   If the soup is too thick, add a little fresh cold milk.

Soúpa Avgolémono

Egg-lemon Soup
Serves 6

6 cups (1.5 litres) chicken stock
   (see p. 140)
65 g (2¼ oz) short-grain rice
4 eggs, well beaten
juice 1-2 lemons

salt
pepper
2 tablespoons finely chopped
   fresh mint

1. Bring the stock to the boil, add the rice and simmer for 15 minutes.
2. Combine the beaten eggs, lemon juice, salt and pepper.
3. Add a ladle of the hot stock to the eggs, beating constantly.
4. Remove the soup from the heat and, while whisking constantly, slowly
   add the egg mixture to it. Adjust the seasoning.
5. Serve hot sprinkled with the mint.

Kreatósoúpa

Greek Beef Soup
Serves 6-8

6 cups (1.5 litres) beef stock
  (see p. 141)
¼ cup (2 oz) rice
1 cup diced cooked meat
  (optional)
4 eggs, separated

salt
juice 1 lemon
freshly ground black pepper

1. Boil 5 cups (1.25 litres) of the stock, then reduce heat, add rice and cook for 20 minutes. Add the meat and simmer for a few minutes.
2. Whip the egg whites and a pinch of salt and while continuing to whip, add egg yolks and lemon juice. Add the remaining cup (8 fl oz) of stock.
3. While stirring constantly over low heat, add this mixture to the soup, stir well until the soup thickens a little. Season to taste.

Fassoulátha

Dried Bean Soup
*From **Pileas Restaurant,** Hania, Mt Pelion*

Serves 6

500 g (1 lb) dried beans
8 cups (2 litres) hot water
¼ cup (2 fl oz) olive oil
2 onions, roughly chopped
3 carrots, roughly chopped
3 stalks celery, sliced
1 cup (8 oz) canned tomatoes,
  peeled and chopped

2 tablespoons tomato paste
2 teaspoons fresh oregano (or 1
  teaspoon dried oregano)
2 bay leaves
salt
freshly ground black pepper

1. Wash the beans and soak them in the water for at least 4 hours.
2. In the olive oil, fry onions, carrots and celery until light brown.
3. Add the tomatoes and tomato paste, oregano and bay leaves.
4. Combine all ingredients including the water in which the beans were soaked, and gently simmer for 2 hours.

Right: Exterior of Pileas Restaurant, Hania, Mt Pelion in the hills above the town of Volos.

Fakkí

Lentil Soup
Serves 6-8

500 g (16 oz) lentils
10 cups (2.5 litres) beef stock
  (see p. 141) or water
½ cup (4 fl oz) olive oil
2 stalks celery, finely chopped
2 large onions, finely chopped
3 sprigs parsley, finely chopped
2 cloves garlic, crushed

2 tablespoons tomato paste
2 bay leaves
1 teaspoon dried oregano
2 tablespoons wine vinegar
freshly ground black pepper
salt

1. Place the lentils in a saucepan, add the beef stock or water, bring to the boil. Take off the heat and soak 30 minutes.
2. In large frying pan, preheat the oil and sauté celery, carrot, onions, parsley and garlic for 10 to 15 minutes.
3. Add tomato paste, bay leaves, oregano and vinegar, cook for a further 5 minutes.
4. Add this mixture to the lentils and beef stock or water. Season to taste and simmer over low heat for 45 minutes. Serve with chunky fresh bread.

Revíthiá Soúpa

Chickpea Soup
Serves 4

350 g (11 oz) dried chickpeas
3 tablespoons olive oil
2 onions, chopped
3 stalks celery, chopped
1 clove garlic

2 sprigs fresh oregano (or ½ teaspoon dried oregano)
5 cups (1.25 litres) water
salt
freshly ground black pepper

1. Soak the chickpeas overnight or boil them in water for 2 minutes and let them soak for 1 hour.
2. Heat the oil in a saucepan and sauté the onions, celery, garlic and oregano until onions are soft and transparent.
3. Add the soaked chickpeas, water and seasoning.
4. Simmer over low heat for 45 minutes or until the chickpeas are very soft. Serve hot.

Kakavia II

Greek Bouillabaisse
Serves 8

½ cup (4 fl oz) olive oil
2 onions, thinly sliced
2 small potatoes, peeled and
  diced
2 small carrots, chopped
1-2 cloves garlic, chopped
4 ripe fresh tomatoes, peeled and
  chopped
8 cups (2 litres) water
1½ teaspoons salt
freshly ground black pepper
2 bay leaves

½ cup (4 fl oz) dry white wine
1.5 kg (3 lb) fish, a mixture of
  2 or 3 types of white
  firm-fleshed fish
½ cup (3 oz) long-grain rice
¼ teaspoon saffron
juice 1 lemon
8 slices of bread for making
  croûtons
60 g (2 oz) butter
8 lemon wedges

1. Heat the oil in a large saucepan and sauté the onions, potatoes, carrots and garlic for 15 minutes.
2. Add the tomatoes and cook for a further 10 minutes.
3. Add water, half the salt, pepper, bay leaves and wine. Simmer for 20 minutes.
4. Wrap the fish in a piece of cheese-cloth approximately 1 metre square. Tie the ends and attach them to a handle, and immerse the pouch in the water. Simmer for 10 minutes.
5. Add rice and simmer for 25 minutes until rice is cooked.
6. Remove the cheese-cloth with the fish and let it cool enough to handle.
7. In the meantime, add the saffron and simmer for 10 minutes.
8. Carefully remove the flesh from the fish bones and return it to the soup.
9. Add lemon juice and season to taste.
10. Make croûtons, by cutting each square slice of bread into four and frying them crisp in butter.
11. Serve the soup hot, with croûtons floating on top and lemon wedges on the side.

SAUCES

Avgolémono is the first name that springs to mind when I think of Greek sauces. I consider it to be one of the true Greek' flavours. Popular with Greek cooks, it is used with lamb, fish, poultry and vegetables, in soups and stews. The smoothness of the thickened egg and acidity of lemon juice are a refreshing combination. It is easy to prepare – as long as, once combined with food, it is not cooked again. There is no way of uncurdling an Avgolémono!

The other sauce that I closely associate with Greek cooking is the pungent garlic-laden Skordaliá, a type of mayonnaise which is used chilled with fish, certain vegetables, and especially as a dip with raw vegetables.

In general in Greek cooking, sauces are a by-product of the cooking process. In fact they are the natural cooking juices of ingredients used. So the number of made-up sauces is very small. The Greeks claim that from their ancient forebears they inherited the Cream Sauce, also known as Béchamel Sauce, and its cheesy version, the Mornay Sauce. Both, of course, are one of the main ingredients of the Moussaká. Most other sauces are simple but strong and savoury, as are most Greek dishes.

Sáltsa Domáta

Tomato Sauce

½ cup (4 fl oz) olive oil
2 onions, finely chopped
1-2 garlic cloves, crushed
1 kg (2 lb) tomatoes, peeled and chopped
4 tablespoons tomato paste

2 bay leaves
1 cup (8 fl oz) dry white wine
1 teaspoon dried basil
1 teaspoon dried oregano
1 teaspoon sugar

1. Heat the oil in a saucepan and sauté the onions and garlic until onions are soft and transparent.
2. Add the remaining ingredients and simmer over low heat for 1 hour. Serve with meatballs, pasta or sausages.

Arvanitia Beach Restaurant, Nafplio

There is hardly a town or village in Greece that has not been founded by some ancient god. Nafplio, on the Peloponnesian Peninsula, is no exception.

The town is said to have been created by Palamides, the son of the sea god Poseidon. Palamides showed good taste in selecting the site, the dark-blue waters of the Bay of Nafplio lap the white sandy beaches, and the imposing rock, the castle of Palamidi and an old Venetian fortress provide an impressive backdrop for the town.

Arvanitia Beach stretches in an arc between the two hills. Overlooking the beach is the Arvanitia Beach Restaurant, quiet and almost deserted in winter but bustling with holidaymakers during the season. Its setting is more imposing than its food; however, the few Greek dishes it includes among the usual international fare are well prepared and tasty.

Right foreground: Veal à la Stanmas with carrots and macaroni; Centre: Eggplant Moussaka (p. 84).

Skorthaliá

Garlic Sauce

This sauce is a type of mayonnaise and is very popular with fried fish or vegetables. The sauce can be made in a food processor, mixer or blender.

Yields 2 cups (16 fl oz)

3 egg yolks
juice 1 lemon
2 tablespoons white wine vinegar
2-5 garlic cloves, crushed
  (according to taste)

1 cup (8 fl oz) olive oil
1 teaspoon salt
90 g (3 oz) blanched almonds,
  finely chopped

1. Place the egg yolks, lemon juice, vinegar and garlic in the food processor container and process for 30 seconds.
2. Add the oil in a slow steady flow and process until thick, smooth and creamy. If too thick, add 1 or 2 tablespoons of water.
3. Transfer into a serving dish or storage container, and mix in the almonds.
4. Refrigerate. Serve with fish or vegetables.

Sáltsa Avgolémono

Egg and Lemon Sauce

Almost a universal sauce in Greece, used in soups and stews, with meat, poultry, fish or vegetables.

Yields 1½ cups (12 fl oz)

3 eggs, separated
salt
1 tablespoon cornflour (optional,
  if thicker sauce is desired)

juice 1 lemon
1½ cups (12 fl oz) chicken stock
  (see p. 140)

1. Beat the egg whites with salt until stiff.
2. Add the egg yolks and lemon juice and beat together.
3. Heat the stock. If using cornflour, mix it to a paste with some water and, while stirring constantly, add it to the stock. Simmer for 2 to 3 minutes.
4. Take the stock off the heat and cool a little. Then while beating continuously, add it to the eggs. Season if necessary.
5. Return it to the heat, continue beating until it thickens. Do not boil.
6. To serve, pour it over the dish for which it is prepared.

Latholémono

Oil and Lemon Sauce

This is a simple lemon-oil dressing which in Greece is used a great deal with cooked and raw vegetables and for the basting of grilled fish, seafood and meat. If made in large quantities it may be stored in the refrigerator for later use.

Yields 1 cup (8 fl oz)

1 cup (8 fl oz) olive oil
juice 1-2 lemons
2 sprigs parsley, finely chopped
4 mint leaves, chopped (optional)

1 teaspoon dried oregano (optional)
salt
freshly ground black pepper

1. In a screw-top jar, combine all ingredients and shake well.
2. If not for immediate use, store in refrigerator.

Kréma

White Cheese Sauce

This is basically a Mornay sauce and the Greeks claim that their forefathers invented it some 2000 years ago.

Makes 4 cups (1 litre)

125 g (4 oz) butter
4 tablespoons flour
4 cups (1 litre) hot milk
salt

¼ teaspoon ground white pepper
¼ teaspoon ground nutmeg
4 tablespoons grated Kefalotíri or Parmesan cheese

1. Melt the butter, add the flour and mix it to a smooth paste. Cook for 5 minutes without colouring it.
2. Take off the heat and, while whisking vigorously, add the milk. Cook over medium heat, stirring constantly for 10 minutes until sauce is smooth and thick.
3. Take off the heat and stir in the remaining ingredients.
4. Use it in Moussaká or Pastítsio. To store, cover with plastic film and refrigerate.

SALADS AND VEGETABLES

In general, salads are not limited to raw green vegetables but also include cooked greens which are served in a lemon or vinegar oil dressing.

Among the most popular vegetables are eggplant (aubergine), okra, zucchini (courgettes) and artichokes. Spinach, tomatoes and beans are also frequently served.

If I were asked which was the most 'Greek' of vegetables, my answer without hesitation would be Melintzána, the everpresent eggplant. Fried or braised, grilled with tomatoes and onions, or served as part of the Moussaká, with herbs, lemons, oil, it reappears in one form or another on every Greek table.

I very much like the way Greeks prepare their vegetables. Cooked with olive oil, herbs (especially oregano) and in combination with other vegetables, the flavour is always strong – they are more like a casserole of vegetables. I also like the care taken with artichokes to preserve their light colour: first rubbed with lemon juice, they are then submerged in water to which cornflour, lemon juice and lemon peel has been added.

Marinating of different types of vegetables is a very typical Greek method of preparation, known internationally as 'à la Grecque'. When using several different vegetables in preparing Vegetables à la Grecque, attention is paid to varying the cooking time, so that all ingredients finish up with the same consistency.

Greeks like their vegetables, and whatever variety is used or whichever way they are prepared, the result is always very tasty.

Restaurant Kuyu, Mikrolimano, Piraeus

Modern Piraeus shows very few traces of its ancient origin. The peninsula across the Saronic Bay from Athens was in its time one of the most important commercial ports and naval bases in the ancient world.

After the decline of Athens as a naval power, Piraeus, for many centuries was just a fishing village. However, since early last century when Athens became the capital of modern Greece, Piraeus has regained its status as the leading port of the country.

One of the most charming parts of Piraeus today is Mikrolimano, the quaint boat harbour, where local fishing boats and elegant yachts are a great setting for some of the best seafood in Greece. The waterfront promenade is lined with seafood restaurants and right at the water's edge, under colourful canvas awnings, the diners enjoy the fresh fish that is offered. It is an international crowd and you can hear many languages spoken.

All the restaurants display a large variety of the sea's bounty. It is all very fresh, as every day the fishermen tie up their boats at Mikrolimano and deliver their catch direct to the restaurants.

A late summer's sunset over the bay is an unforgettable occasion and if the day is clear, you can see the Acropolis of Athens in the distance.

Right: Clockwise from bottom left: Stuffed Peppers (p. 80); Octopus Salad (p. 14); Mussels Plaki; Rice-stuffed vine leaves (p. 12); Taramosalata (p. 13) and centre: Prawns with Feta Cheese (p. 60).

Imám Bayildí

Braised Eggplant with Onions and Tomatoes
*From **Costoyanis Taverna**, Athens.*

The name means 'the Imam fainted' and the dish is known throughout the Middle East and many claim its origin. The legend is that the Imam swooned when he scented its fine fragrance. Served as an appetiser or main course.

Serves 6

3 long eggplants (aubergine), each weighing 500 g (1 lb)
salt
4 onions, cut in half and sliced
2 cloves garlic
½ cup (4 fl oz) olive oil
5 large firm ripe tomatoes, peeled and chopped or 500 g (2 cups) drained canned tomatoes, chopped

4 sprigs parsley, chopped
freshly ground black pepper
juice 1 lemon
1 teaspoon sugar
½ cup (4 fl oz) water
3 sprigs parsley, chopped, for garnish

1. Cut off the stem and peel each eggplant lengthways, leaving alternate strips of skin about 2.5 cm (1 in) wide.
2. Cut each eggplant in half. Into the cut side, make 3 or 4 long incisions.
3. Sprinkle these sides with salt. Place them, salted side down, in a shallow dish and pour in enough water to cover and let stand for 30 minutes.
4. Over a low heat, fry the onions and garlic in half of the oil until soft and transparent.
5. In a bowl combine the onions and garlic tomatoes and parsley. Season to taste.
6. Remove the eggplant from the water, squeeze the pieces gently and dry them with a paper towel.
7. Using an oven dish or casserole large enough to contain the eggplant in one layer, fry them lightly on both sides in the remaining oil.
8. Arrange them with the cut side up and force the onion-tomato mixture into the cuts and heap the rest in equal amounts on each.
9. Sprinkle each with the lemon juice and sugar, and spoon some of the oil on top.
10. Add ½ cup of water to the dish, bring to the boil then reduce the heat, cover and simmer for one hour, basting occasionally with the cooking juices. If necessary, add more water.
11. To serve, spoon the cooking juices over them and garnish with parsley.

Kolokithákia Tiganitá

Fried Zucchini

Eggplant, by far the most popular vegetable in Greece, can also be prepared in this manner.

Serves 4

4 zucchini (courgettes), cut into 1 cm (¼ in) slices
salt
½ cup (2 oz) flour

oil for frying
freshly ground black pepper

1. Place the zucchini slices in a sieve or colander and sprinkle with salt. Let this stand for 30 minutes to drain excess water.
2. Rinse the zucchini and dry with a teatowel or paper towel.
3. Dip the zucchini slices in the flour and fry golden brown in hot oil.
4. Drain on a paper towel and serve hot, seasoned with pepper.

Fassoulákia me Domátes

Green Beans with Tomatoes
Serves 6

750 g (1½ lb) fresh French beans
1 teaspoon salt
¼ cup (2 fl oz) olive oil
2 onions, finely chopped
½ clove garlic, crushed
6 fresh ripe tomatoes, peeled and chopped

2 teaspoons red or white wine vinegar
1 teaspoon dried or 2 teaspoons fresh oregano, chopped
1 teaspoon dried or 2 teaspoons fresh marjoram, chopped
salt
freshly ground black pepper

1. Top and tail and if necessary string the beans.
2. Bring a large pan of water to the boil, add the salt and beans and boil for 8 minutes.
3. Drain the water and rinse the beans in running cold water in a colander.
4. In a frying pan, heat the oil and lightly fry the onions and garlic until the onions are soft and transparent.
5. Add the tomatoes, vinegar, oregano and marjoram and simmer for 10 minutes.
6. Add the beans and simmer for a further 5 minutes. Season with salt and pepper and serve hot as a vegetable with a meat dish.

Saláta

Greek Salad

*This salad was served to me at the **Marmara Restaurant** in Mistras and it contains most of the ingredients that Greeks may use in their salads. However, to these ingredients you may add lettuce, tender spinach or dandelion leaves, sliced radishes or celery, capers or zucchini, or any combination of ingredients available at the time.*

Serves 6

3 firm ripe tomatoes, cut into wedges
2 cucumbers, peeled and sliced
3 green peppers (capsicums), seeded and cut into strips
2 onions, roughly chopped
6 fillets of anchovies
12 Kalamata olives
250 g (8 oz) feta cheese, cut into 1.5 cm (¾ in) cubes

Dressing:
½ cup (4 fl oz) olive oil
⅓ cup (3 fl oz) white or red wine vinegar
1 clove garlic, crushed
2 tablespoons finely chopped dill
1 teaspoon fresh (or dried) oregano
½ teaspoon salt
freshly ground black pepper

1. In a salad bowl combine all the vegetables.
2. To prepare the dressing, combine the ingredients in a watertight screw-top jar, shake vigorously, taste for seasoning.
3. Pour the dressing over the salad and toss.
4. On top arrange the anchovies and olives and sprinkle with feta.

Fassoúlia Saláta

Bean Salad
Serves 6-8

500 g (1 lb) dried beans
¾ cup (6 fl oz) olive oil
juice 2 lemons
1 teaspoon salt

freshly ground black pepper
2 onions, finely chopped
3 sprigs parsley, finely chopped

1. Boil the beans for a few minutes and let them stand for 1 hour.
2. Add more water, bring to the boil, cover and simmer for 1-1½ hours until tender but still firm. Drain.
3. In a screw-top jar, mix the dressing of oil, lemon juice, salt and pepper.
4. Mix the onions into the still-hot beans, and toss with the dressing.
5. Refrigerate for 2 hours. Serve garnished with parsley.

Right: Herod Atticus Odeon at the foot of the Acropolis, Athens.

Melitzanosaláta

Eggplant Salad
Serves 6

3-4 eggplants (aubergine), 1 kg (2 lb) in total weight
1 onion, grated
1 garlic clove, crushed
1 large firm ripe tomato, peeled and finely chopped
1 green pepper (capsicum), seeded and chopped

2 sprigs dill, chopped
¾ cup (6 fl oz) olive oil
juice 1-1½ lemons (according to taste)
salt
freshly ground black pepper
12 black olives for garnish

1. Preheat the oven to 200° C (400° F/Gas 6).
2. Bake the eggplant in the preheated oven for about 1 hour until skins are black and the flesh is soft.
3. Allow to cool, then skin the eggplant and chop the flesh very fine.
4. Add all the ingredients, decorate with black olives and refrigerate before serving with roasted, grilled or fried meats or fish.

Portokália me Eliés

Orange and Black Olive Salad
An unusual but very tasty combination of flavours.

Serves 6

1 small onion, thinly sliced
3 large oranges, peeled and thinly sliced, seeds discarded
24 large black olives, pitted
3 tablespoons olive oil

juice ½ lemon
salt
freshly ground black pepper
6 lettuce leaves
3 sprigs parsley, finely chopped

1. Blanch the sliced onion in boiling water for 1 minute.
2. In a bowl, combine blanched onion, oranges, olives.
3. In a screw-top jar, combine oil, lemon juice, salt and pepper. Shake well and pour it over the oranges.
4. Refrigerate for 6 hours. Serve on lettuce leaves, sprinkled with parsley.

Pepperiés Orektiká

Marinated Capsicum Salad
Serves 4

4 green peppers (capsicums)
4 spring onions (scallions), finely chopped
3 tablespoons olive oil
juice 1 lemon

1 teaspoon white wine vinegar
½ teaspoon oregano, chopped
salt
freshly ground black pepper

1. Preheat the oven to 200° C (400° F/Gas 6).
2. Bake the green peppers (capsicums) for 30 minutes or until the skin blisters.
3. Cut them into halves, remove seeds and then cut them into 1-1.5 cm (½ in) strips.
4. In a screw-top jar, combine the remaining ingredients, shake well and pour over the green pepper strips.
5. Refrigerate. Serve at room temperature as a salad or first course.

Omelétta me Patátes ke Domátes

Potato, Tomato and Onion Omelette
Serves 4

90 g (3 oz) butter
1 onion, chopped
1 green pepper (capsicum), seeded and chopped
2 tomatoes, peeled and roughly chopped
1 potato, cubed

6 eggs
salt
freshly ground black pepper
1 tablespoon water
60 g (2 oz) feta cheese, crumbled
2 sprigs parsley, chopped

1. In half of the butter, lightly fry the onions and green pepper (capsicum) for 5 minutes. Add the tomatoes and fry for a further 2 to 3 minutes.
2. Remove with a slotted spoon and set aside.
3. Add the rest of the butter to the frying pan and fry the potatoes for 20 minutes or until they are crisp and brown.
4. While the potatoes are frying, whip the eggs until fluffy and add salt, pepper and the water. Use little salt as the feta will also add some saltiness.
5. Add the onions and green pepper to the frying pan and mix with the potatoes.
6. Heat and pour the egg mix over the vegetables. Cook until the eggs set, do not fold. To serve, slide on to a heated serving dish.

Lahana Marináta

Marinated Vegetables à la Grecque
Any one or any combination of vegetables may be used. Note, the different vegetables require different cooking times and should be cooked separately. Recommended cooking times are given in brackets.

Serves 6

Marinade:
1 cup (8 fl oz) dry white wine
8 cups (2 litres) water
¾ cup (6 fl oz) olive oil
juice 3 lemons
3 teaspoons salt
1 garlic clove, crushed
10 sprigs parsley, roughly chopped
1 stalk celery, chopped
1 stalk fennel, chopped
2 sprigs fresh thyme, chopped
10 peppercorns
10 coriander seeds, cracked

Vegetables (1 kg serves 6):
pickling-type onions, peeled (20 min)
green peppers (capsicums), seeded, cut in strips (10 min)
button mushrooms, caps only (5 min)
cucumbers, peeled, seeded, cut into strips (5 min)
zucchini, cut into 4 lengthways (10 min)
cauliflower, broken up into flowerets (8 min)
carrots, cut lengthways into strips (15 min)

1. In a large saucepan combine all marinade ingredients, bring to the boil and simmer for 1 hour.
2. Strain through a sieve and press the solids to extract all the flavour.
3. Prepare vegetables and simmer each vegetable separately in marinade until tender. If 'al dente' texture is desired, use shorter cooking times.
4. Remove with slotted spoon and arrange on a china or glass serving dish.
5. Boil marinade until reduced to 1 cup (8 fl oz). Taste, and season if necessary.
6. Pour over vegetables, cool and refrigerate for 12 hours. Serve at room temperature.

Right: The monument of the Ship of the Argonauts in the Volos.

Kounoupithi Tiyanito

Crumbed Fried Cauliflower
A dish from Macedonia.

Serves 6

1½ teaspoons salt
1 tablespoon vinegar
1 lemon
1 medium-sized cauliflower,
  broken up into neat flowerets
2 eggs

½ cup (4 fl oz) milk
salt
freshly ground black pepper
125 g (4 oz) dry breadcrumbs
½ cup (4 fl oz) olive oil

1. In a large saucepan, boil water, add salt and vinegar, cut the lemon in half and squeeze the juice, add the juice and the squeezed-out halves to the pan, add the cauliflower, and boil for 10 to 15 minutes depending on the texture required.
2. Drain and rinse the cauliflower under running cold water.
3. Beat the eggs, add milk, salt and pepper.
4. Dip the flowerets first in the egg mixture and then in the breadcrumbs.
5. Fry in hot oil until brown. Drain on kitchen paper and serve hot.

Saláta Kolokithákia

Zucchini Salad with Almonds
This dish may be served as a cold salad with cold meat or warm with fried fish.

Serves 4

500 g (1 lb) zucchini (courgettes)
salt
freshly ground black pepper
¼ cup (2 fl oz) olive oil

1 tablespoon wine vinegar, or
  juice 1 lemon
60 g (2 oz) blanched roasted
  almonds
3 sprigs parsley, finely chopped

1. Boil the zucchini (courgettes) in boiling salted water for 10 minutes. Drain and when cool enough to handle slice into 1 cm (⅓ in) slices.
2. In a screw-top jar, mix salt, pepper, oil, vinegar or lemon juice. Pour over the zucchini. Mix in the almonds.
3. Serve warm, or refrigerate and serve as a cold salad, sprinkled with parsley.

Lahana sto Fourno

Vegetable Casserole

This dish is the Greek version of the French ratatouille. In Greece it is served as a vegetable dish with meats or as a Lenten main-course dish.

Serves 4

1 onion, sliced

4 large tomatoes, peeled and quartered

1 potato, peeled and cut into large cubes

250 g (8 oz) fresh beans, cut into 2.5 cm (1 in) pieces

250 g (8 oz) eggplant (aubergine), cubed

2 green peppers (capsicums), seeded and roughly chopped

2 zucchini (courgettes), cut into slices

2 stalks celery, sliced

1-2 garlic cloves, crushed (according to taste)

3 sprigs parsley, chopped

3 sprigs dill, chopped

1-2 teaspoons salt

freshly ground black pepper

½ cup (4 fl oz) oil

water

1. Preheat the oven to 180° C (350° F/Gas 4).
2. In a casserole combine all ingredients and add enough water to cover.
3. Bring to boil on the stove. Cover with lid and cook in the preheated oven for 1½ hours. Serve hot.

Angináres Piláfi

Artichoke Pilaf
Serves 4

4 large or 8 small artichokes

½ cup (2 oz) cornflour (cornstarch)

salt

juice 1 lemon

1 onion, finely chopped

45 g (1½ oz) butter

1 tablespoon tomato paste

salt

freshly ground black pepper

water

1¼ cups (6 oz) long-grain rice

90 g (3 oz) feta cheese, crumbled

1. Prepare and cook artichokes in accordance with the recipe for Angináres me Avgolémono on p. 57. Cut each into 4 and set aside.
2. In a saucepan, fry the onion in the butter until soft and transparent.
3. Add tomato paste, salt, pepper and enough water to cook the rice.
4. Bring to boil and add rice. Simmer. After 10 minutes add the artichokes and continue simmering until the rice is cooked.
5. Take off the heat and gently stir in the feta cheese. Serve hot.

49

Fassoúlia

Greek Haricot Beans
Serves 4

250 g (8 oz) dry haricot beans
½ cup (4 fl oz) olive oil
1 clove garlic, crushed
2 bay leaves
2 sprigs thyme, chopped
1 tablespoon tomato paste

enough boiling water to cover beans by 2.5 cm (1 in)
juice 1 lemon
1 onion, sliced into rings
salt
freshly ground black pepper

1. Soak the beans in water overnight.
2. In a saucepan heat the oil and add the strained beans.
3. Over low heat simmer them for 10 minutes.
4. Add the garlic, bay leaves, thyme, tomato paste and boiling water.
5. Cook them over low heat for 3 hours.
6. Add the lemon juice, onion, salt and pepper. Serve at room temperature.

Prasa Marináta

Leeks à la Grecque
Serves 4

8-12 small leeks, white parts only
salt
1 teaspoon cornflour (cornstarch)

juice 1 lemon
1 tablespoon oil
freshly ground black pepper

1. Boil the leeks in salted water until they are soft.
2. Drain off most of the water leaving enough to cover the leeks.
3. Dissolve the cornflour in some water and add it to the leeks.
4. Stir and cook until sauce thickens.
5. Add lemon juice and oil and mix in well. Season and serve warm.

Right: Olympus Naoussa Restaurant, Thessaloniki.

Patáto Keftédes

Potato Balls
Serves 4-6

1 kg (2 lb) potatoes, boiled and
   peeled
30 g (1 oz) butter, melted
salt
freshly ground black pepper
3 sprigs parsley, chopped

3 spring onions (scallions),
   chopped
4 tomatoes, peeled and finely
   chopped
1 cup (4 oz) flour
oil for frying

1. Mash the potatoes, add all the ingredients and mix well and knead lightly.
2. With your hands dusted with a little flour, roll the mixture into balls and then flatten them into rounds.
3. In a frying pan, heat the oil and fry them until they are golden brown.

Angináres a la Polita

Artichokes with Dill Sauce
Serves 6

juice 2-3 lemons
3 tablespoons (1 oz) cornflour
   (cornstarch)
1¼ cups (10 fl oz) water
6 medium-to-large artichokes
1 cup (8 fl oz) olive oil

1 onion, finely chopped
3 tablespoons fresh chopped dill
1 teaspoon salt
freshly ground black pepper

1. Mix the lemon juice, cornflour and water together, set aside.
2. Trim off the stalks of the artichokes, leaving 2.5-5 cm (1-2 in) of stalk on the artichokes. Remove all discoloured leaves.
3. Lay each artichoke on its side and cut 2.5-4 cm (1-1½ in) off the tips of the leaves. Rub all cut surfaces with lemon juice.
4. Drop the artichokes into the lemon-cornflour mixture to soak.
5. Heat the oil in a large saucepan or casserole.
6. Add the onion and sauté for 5 minutes.
7. With a slotted spoon, remove the artichokes from the lemon-cornflour mixture and set them aside. Pour the mixture into the saucepan or casserole and, while stirring constantly, bring it to the boil.
8. Add the dill, salt and pepper and then put the artichokes in.
9. Cover and simmer for 35 to 40 minutes, turning the artichokes once.
10. Serve the artichokes at room temperature with the sauce poured over them.

Domatorizo Piláfi

Tomato Pilaf
Serves 4

2 large ripe tomatoes, peeled and
   chopped
60 g (2 oz) butter
1 teaspoon salt
freshly ground black pepper

1¾ cup (14 fl oz) beef stock
   (see p.141)
1 tablespoon tomato purée
225 g (7 oz) rice
3 tablespoons (60 g) melted
   butter

1. In a heavy saucepan, cook tomatoes, butter, salt, pepper, beef stock and tomato purée until it reduces to approximately 2 cups (16 fl oz).
2. Add the rice, stir in well, cover and simmer for about 20 minutes, until the liquid has been absorbed and the rice is tender but not too soft.
3. Add the melted butter and stir it in with a fork.
4. Cover the saucepan with a teatowel and let it stand for 20 minutes before serving.

Rízi Piláfi

Plain Rice Pilaf
Serves 4

45 g (1½ oz) butter
1½ cups (8 oz) long-grain rice
1 onion, finely chopped

3 cups (24 fl oz) chicken stock
   (see p. 140) or water
salt
⅛ teaspoon saffron (optional)

1. In the butter, lightly sauté the rice and onions for 5 minutes.
2. Add stock or water, and salt (and saffron, if desired). Bring to the boil and under cover, undisturbed, simmer over low heat for 20 to 25 minutes.

Domátes Yemistés

Stuffed Tomatoes
Serves 4

8 large firm tomatoes
1 tablespoon sugar
salt
3 tablespoons olive oil
1 large onion, finely chopped
1 clove garlic, crushed
500 g (1 lb) minced beef or lamb
1 teaspoon salt
freshly ground black pepper

¼ cup (2 oz) long-grain rice, parboiled
½ teaspoon dried mint or 2 sprigs fresh mint, chopped
½ cup dry red wine
¼ cup (1 oz) dry breadcrumbs
2 tablespoons grated Kefalotíri or Parmesan cheese
2 cups tomato sauce (see p. 34)

1. Preheat the oven to 180°C (350°F /Gas 4).
2. Cut a slice off the top of each tomato and save it for use later as a lid.
3. With a teaspoon, scoop out the pulp, chop it and save for use in the stuffing.
4. Sprinkle the inside of the tomatoes with sugar and salt and place them upside down on a rack to drain.
5. In a large frying pan, heat the oil and sauté the onion and garlic until the onion is soft and transparent.
6. Add the minced meat and mix well with the back of a fork until it is broken up. Fry until it is brown.
7. Add reserved tomato pulp, salt, pepper, rice, mint and wine.
8. Simmer over low heat for 20 minutes, stirring occasionally. Add more wine or water if the mixture gets too dry.
9. Remove from heat and let it cool.
10. With a teaspoon, fill the tomatoes with the mixture.
11. Sprinkle the top with breadcrumbs and cheese, and cover with the tomato lids.
12. Place the tomatoes in a baking dish and pour the tomato sauce between them.
13. Place in the preheated oven and bake for 15 to 20 minutes, occasionally remove the caps and baste with the sauce. Serve hot or lukewarm with the sauce poured over the tomatoes.

Right: One of the many colourful wayside shrines so typical of the Greek countryside.

Kolokithákia sto Fourno

Baked Zucchini
Serves 6

4 large tomatoes, peeled and
   chopped
1 clove garlic, crushed
½ cup (4 fl oz) olive oil
1 teaspoon sugar
½ teaspoon oregano
½ teaspoon mint
salt

freshly ground black pepper
1 kg (2 lb) zucchini (courgettes),
   cut lengthways into 1 cm (¼ in)
   slices
2 onions, sliced
½ cup (2 oz) dry breadcrumbs
125 g (4 oz) feta cheese, cut into
   small cubes
30 g (1 oz) butter

1. Preheat the oven to 180° C (350° F/Gas 4).
2. Combine tomatoes, garlic, oil, sugar, oregano, mint, salt and pepper.
3. In an oiled baking dish, arrange layers of zucchini, tomato mixture and
   onion slices.
4. Sprinkle the top with breadcrumbs and cheese, and dot it with butter.
5. Bake in the preheated oven for 45 minutes until zucchini is tender.

Angináres ki Koukia

Broad Beans and Artichokes
Serves 4-6

8 artichokes
3 tablespoons (1 oz) cornflour
   (cornstarch)
juice 2 lemons
500 g (1 lb) fresh broad beans,
   shelled
salt
2 tablespoons vinegar

2 tablespoons olive oil
1 teaspoon cornflour (cornstarch)
½ cup (4 fl oz) water in which
   beans were cooked
3 sprigs parsley, chopped
freshly ground black pepper

1. Cook the artichokes with the lemon juice and cornflour according to the
   recipe on p. 57.
2. Remove all leaves from the artichokes and cut off the stalks.
3. Cook the beans in salted water until they are tender. Drain, but keep ½
   cup (4 fl oz) of the water for later use.
4. Heat the oil in a saucepan, add the teaspoon of cornflour, the ½ cup of
   bean cooking water, parsley and seasoning.
5. Cook for a few minutes until the sauce thickens, add the beans and
   artichoke bottoms and serve hot. A few drops of lemon juice will
   improve the flavour.

Angináres me Avgolémono

Artichokes with Egg-lemon Sauce
Serves 6

12 large artichokes
½ cup (2 oz) cornflour (cornstarch)
salt

juice 2 lemons
1½ cups (12 fl oz) egg-lemon sauce (see p. 36)
3 sprigs dill, finely chopped

1. Wash the artichokes and trim each one by breaking off all the coarse outer leaves.
2. Cut the stalk at a point where it breaks easily. Leave the remainder of the stalk on the artichoke as it will be tender and edible.
3. Lay the artichoke on its side and cut 2.5-4 cm (1-1½ in) off the tips of the leaves. Rub the cut surfaces with some of the lemon juice.
4. Dissolve the cornflour in 4 cups (1 litre) of water, add the remaining lemon juice and place the artichokes in this as soon as they are trimmed. This will prevent discolouration.
5. Strain the artichokes and put the liquid into a large saucepan. Add enough fresh water to cover the artichokes and bring to the boil. Add the artichokes, cover them with a teatowel and place a lid on the pan.
6. Boil for approximately 25 minutes or until tender. Remove them from the pan with a slotted spoon and rinse under cold water.
7. Gently part the leaves and remove and discard the choke.
8. Place them on a serving platter.
9. Prepare the egg-lemon sauce, using chicken stock, in accordance with the recipe on p. 36.
10. To serve, pour the sauce over the artichokes and sprinkle with dill.

Patátes tis Katsarolas

Braised Potatoes
Serves 6

¼ cup (4 fl oz) olive oil
750 g (1½ lb) potatoes, peeled and quartered
2 onions, sliced
1 garlic clove, crushed

500 g (1 lb) fresh tomatoes, peeled and roughly chopped
salt
freshly ground black pepper

1. In a heavy-bottomed saucepan, heat the oil and fry the potatoes, onions and garlic until light brown.
2. Add tomatoes and seasoning.
3. Cover and simmer for 30 minutes.
4. Serve hot as a vegetable dish with meat or poultry.

FISH

With the Aegean Sea to the east, the Ionian Sea to the west and the Mediterranean to the south, it's not surprising that fish and seafood of different types have been, since ancient times, important sources of nourishment. Pottery vases some 4000 years old, dating back to the Minoan civilisation of Crete, depict fish and fishermen. So the traditions of preparing fish are really well established.

Greeks claim that the bouillabaisse of Marseilles is of Greek origin, that it was adopted from the Ionians who in the 6th century BC colonised Massilia (the ancient Marseilles), and the Ionian Kakavia became the now-famous bouillabaisse. It is interesting to note that the names of both are derived from the vessels in which the fish was prepared.

Today, everywhere you go in Greece, you will find good fresh fish, especially along the sea shores – though even inland, which is never too far from the seas.

Greek cooking is cooking by peasants and fishermen and therefore local fish and seafood dishes are never sophisticated. They are always full of rich and hearty flavours. Most of them are simple to prepare and good to eat with plenty of chunky fresh bread and lots of local wine. Among internationally known seafood of Greece is the grey mullet roe; salted, dried, coated with wax, it is sold as Botago. Sliced, it is eaten as an hors d'oeuvre on pieces of toast. The same roe is also used in the preparation in one of the favourite of Mezéthes, the Taramosaláta.

The sparkling, clear blue waters that surround Corfu yield the famous spiny lobster. So popular is it that most of it is exported and what little is available locally is priced out of reach of ordinary mortals.

Every town and village along the coastline of the mainland and the islands has its waterfront tavernas and restaurants, and it is there where you will find true Greek seafood.

Olympos Naoussa Restaurant, Thessaloniki

Thessaloniki, named after the sister of Alexander the Great, today has only few reminders of its ancient past. In Roman days it was the capital city of the province of Macedonia but today only a few ruins bear witness of its important past.

As the second-largest city of Greece it is the most important city in Northern Greece.

The people of Thessaloniki like to eat well and there are numerous good restaurants serving Greek food. The Olympos Naoussa Restaurant is among the best in town and its owner Aristotelis Sfikas, ably assisted by his manager Takis Carayiannis, offer a wide variety of Greek dishes: veal stew with squashes, fried mussels, spinach risotto, red snapper baked in the oven à la Spetisiota, shrimp with mayonnaise, and rice with mussels.

The restaurant is spacious, with high ceilings and during the midday meal the place is filled with spirited conversation. Waiters shout their orders and the clinking of dishes adds to the general noise. It is all part of the typical atmosphere of a busy Greek restaurant.

Right: Clockwise from centre foreground: Veal Stew and Squashes; Fried Mussels; Snapper à la Spetiota; Prawn Mayonnaise; Rice with Mussels. Centre: Rice with Spinach.

Garíthes me Fétta

Prawns with Feta Cheese

*At the **Kuyu Restaurant** along the Mikrolimana at Piraeus, this dish goes under the modest name of Shrimp Casserole. It is simple but delicious. I have tried my own version of this dish in which I substituted the prawns with pieces of fish. I have also used oysters and scallops, added at the last moment. Any seafood, such as mussels or crayfish pieces could be used. I have also tried retsina instead of dry white wine and achieved an added flavour.*

Serves 4 as a main course dish or 6 as a first course.

1 onion, chopped
1 garlic clove, crushed
3 tablespoons olive oil
8 large ripe peeled tomatoes, fresh or canned, roughly chopped (if using canned tomatoes, use the liquid as well)
2 tablespoons tomato paste
½ cup (4 fl oz) dry white wine (or retsina)

1 teaspoon dried oregano
4 sprigs parsley, chopped
salt
freshly ground black pepper
125 g (4 oz) feta cheese, cut into 2.5 cm (1 in) cubes
16-20 king prawns, green, shelled and de-veined

1. Lightly fry the onion and garlic in the oil until the onion is transparent and soft.
2. Add the tomatoes (and liquid, if using canned tomatoes), tomato paste, wine and oregano.
3. Simmer for 20 to 30 minutes until some of the liquid has evaporated and the mixture has the texture of a thick sauce.
4. Add the parsley and season to taste.
5. Add the feta and the prawns, and continue cooking for 2 to 3 minutes – long enough to cook the prawns and heat the feta. If cooked too long, the prawns will be tough and the feta will melt too much.
6. Serve hot, with chunky pieces of fresh white bread and wash down with a glass of chilled retsina.

Garíthes Piláfi

Prawn Pilaf

This is an adaptation of the Greek recipe, as I do not agree with the method that requires the precooking of prawns (which only need the barest of heat).

Serves 4

16-24 uncooked prawns, depending on size
8 cups (2 litres) water
1 stalk celery, chopped
1 carrot, chopped
2 onions, chopped
6 peppercorns
3 bay leaves
½ teaspoon chopped oregano
2 tablespoons olive oil
½ clove garlic, crushed
3 ripe tomatoes, peeled and chopped

2 tablespoons tomato purée
1 green pepper (capsicum), seeded and roughly chopped
1 cup (5 oz) long-grain rice
4 cups (1 litre) prawn stock (from steps 1-6, below)
salt
freshly ground black pepper
12 olives for garnish
grated Kefalotíri or Parmesan cheese (optional)

1. In a large saucepan, using all the water, simmer the celery, carrot, 1 of the chopped onions, peppercorns, bay leaves and oregano for 30 minutes.
2. In the meantime, peel the uncooked prawns, putting the shells and heads aside.
3. With a sharp knife, make an incision in the back of the prawns and de-vein them.
4. Rinse the prawns under cold water and cut each into 2-3 pieces. Set these aside.
5. To the vegetables in the saucepan, add the prawn shells and heads, mix well together. Cover and simmer gently for 20 minutes.
6. Remove from heat and let it cool for 20 to 30 minutes. Then strain the prawn stock. (Four cups of this stock will need to be heated for use in step 9.)
7. Heat the oil and sauté the second chopped onion and the garlic until the onion is soft and transparent.
8. Add the tomatoes, tomato purée and green pepper (capsicum). Cook for 5 minutes.
9. Stir in the rice. Add strained heated prawn stock. Season.
10. Cover the saucepan, reduce the heat to low, and simmer for 20 minutes without taking off the lid.
11. Stir in the chopped prawns, cover the saucepan and continue to simmer for 5 minutes.
12. Take off the heat and let stand for 10 minutes. Taste and season if necessary. Serve garnished with black olives and if desired sprinkled with grated Kefalotíri or Parmesan cheese.

Garíthes Souvlákia

Grilled Prawn Skewers

This is a delicious way of preparing prawns. As in many Greek dishes, the natural flavour of the basic ingredients is enhanced through the process of marinating in oil, lemon juice and herbs (especially oregano).

Serves 6

½ cup (4 fl oz) olive oil
juice 3 lemons
1 tablespoon fresh oregano, chopped, or 1 teaspoon dried oregano

½ teaspoon salt
freshly ground black pepper
1 kg (2 lb) fresh king prawns, unshelled

1. To prepare the marinade, combine all ingredients except prawns in a screw-top jar and shake well.
2. Place the prawns in an enamelled or glass dish, and pour the marinade over them.
3. Refrigerate for 4 hours.
4. Preheat the griller.
5. Divide the prawns into 6 portions and place them on 6 metal or bamboo skewers.
6. Place them under the preheated griller, baste frequently with the marinade, and grill them for 2 minutes, then turn them and grill for a further 2 minutes.
7. When serving, pour the rest of the marinade over the prawns and serve in their shells.

Right: Monastery, Paleokastritsa, Corfu.

Míthia Piláfi

Mussel Pilaf
Serves 4

48 mussels, washed
1 cup (8 fl oz) dry white wine
3 cups (24 fl oz) water
1 clove garlic, crushed
5 sprigs parsley, finely chopped

½ cup (4 fl oz) olive oil
2 onions, chopped
2 cups (12 oz) rice
salt
freshly ground black pepper

1. Place the mussels, wine, water, garlic and parsley in a saucepan and bring it to the boil. Simmer over low heat until the mussel shells open.
2. Strain and reserve the liquid. Take the mussels (except a few for garnish) out of their shells, and set them aside.
3. Heat the oil in a saucepan and sauté the onions until golden. Add the rice and cook for 2 minutes.
4. In a separate pan bring the mussel liquid to the boil and pour it on to the rice, enough to just cover it. Season.
5. Bring to the boil, then reduce heat and slowly simmer it for 20 minutes until liquid is absorbed.
6. Take off the heat and stir in the mussels. Let it stand for 10 minutes before serving. Serve sprinkled with parsley and garnished with the few cooked mussels still in their shells.

Athenaiki

Fish with Prawns and Mayonnaise
Serves 4

1 kg (2 lb) fish fillets, steamed
  and allowed to cool
250 g (8 oz) small prawns,
  cooked, shelled and cooled
1 small onion, finely chopped
1 tablespoon capers

1½ cups (12 fl oz) mayonnaise,
  (see p. 141)
salt
freshly ground black pepper
2 sprigs parsley, finely chopped
12 black olives

1. With the back of a fork, flake the fish fillets.
2. In a bowl, combine fish, prawns, onion, capers, ½ cup (4 fl oz) of the mayonnaise, salt and pepper. Mix well together.
3. On a decorative round serving platter, form the fish mixture into a mound, coat it with the remainder of the mayonnaise, sprinkle with parsley and garnish with olives. Refrigerate for 1 hour before serving.

Psári Vrastó

Steamed Fish
Serves 4-6

6 small potatoes, peeled
2 carrots, sliced
3 stalks celery, chopped
6 small onions, peeled
1 clove garlic, chopped
3 tablespoons olive oil
1 cup (8 fl oz) dry white wine
salt
freshly ground black pepper
1.5 kg (3 lb) snapper or bream,
   fillets cut into 5 cm (2 in)
   pieces
juice 1 lemon

Sauce:
3 tablespoons olive oil
juice 1 lemon
2 sprigs parsley, chopped
salt
freshly ground black pepper

1. In a saucepan, place the potatoes, carrots, celery, onions, garlic, olive oil, freshly ground black pepper, wine and salt and pepper. Cover, bring to the boil and simmer for 15 minutes.
2. Season the fish with salt and pepper and arrange the pieces on top of the vegetables. Pour the lemon juice over the fish, cover the pan and simmer for a further 15 minutes until potatoes are cooked.
3. To make the sauce, combine ingredients in a screw-top jar and shake well together.
4. To serve, place the fish pieces in the centre of a hot serving plate and arrange the vegetables around them. Serve hot with oil-and-lemon sauce.

Psári Bouryetto

Braised Fish
Serves 4

1 kg (2 lb) snapper or any
   white-fleshed fish fillets
salt
freshly ground black pepper
juice 2 lemons

½ cup (4 fl oz) olive oil
½ teaspoon dry oregano
3 sprigs parsley, chopped

1. Place the fish on a large dish.
2. Combine salt, pepper, lemon juice, oil and oregano and pour it over the fish. Refrigerate for 2 hours.
3. Transfer the fish and marinade to a large saucepan or lidded frying pan. Cover and braise over low heat for 10 minutes.
4. Serve with the cooking liquid and sprinkled with parsley.

Psári Ladorigano

Fish with Tomatoes, Wine and Oregano
From **Metaftsis Restaurant**, *Volos.*

Serves 6

6 fish cutlets, 2.5 cm (1 in) thick
  (use jewfish, snapper or any
  firm white-fleshed fish)
salt
freshly ground black pepper
juice 1 lemon
250 g (1 cup) canned peeled
  tomatoes, chopped
3 tablespoons tomato purée

½ cup (4 fl oz) dry white wine
½ cup (4 fl oz) olive oil
1 clove garlic, chopped
2 teaspoons dried oregano
3 fresh tomatoes, peeled and
  sliced
3 sprigs parsley, chopped

1. Preheat the oven to 200° C (400° F/Gas 6).
2. Arrange the fish cutlets in a baking dish 5 cm (2 in) deep. Sprinkle with salt, pepper and lemon juice.
3. In a saucepan, combine the rest of the ingredients except the fresh tomato slices and parsley. Simmer on slow heat for 30 minutes.
4. Pour the sauce over the fish, arrange the fresh tomato slices on top, and sprinkle with parsley.
5. Place the baking dish in the preheated oven and cook for 30 minutes. Serve hot.

Hotel Amalia, Olympia

The newly built modern Hotel Amalia is a comfortable base from which to explore the west coast of the Peloponnesian Peninsula, with its string of beaches along the picturesque shore.

As at most tourist hotels, in addition to Greek dishes there is a wide range of international dishes on the menu and I consider it a pity that more local and more typical dishes are not prepared.

The Hotel is situated not far from the archeological site of Olympia, the home of the Olympic Games of antiquity. Today, ruins mark what was once the centre of the Hellenic world. It was here that representatives of all the Hellenic city-states gathered to compete in friendly, yet competitive athletic combat. During the brief period of truce while the games were conducted, the spirit of Hellenic unity was forged.

Among the ruins, many important ancient sculptures were found, the most important being that of Hermes by Praxiteles whose workshop was part of the Olympic complex. The sculptures, which also include those of the two pediments of the Temple of Zeus, are among the greatest examples of ancient Greece and can be seen in the two museums at Olympia.

Right: From bottom: Tiropetes (p. 16); Greek Salad (p. 42); Greek Meat Balls (p. 82); Beans à la Piaz. Also in picture are dishes of cold meats and a display of Greek wines.

Psári Lemonato sto Fourno

Baked Fish with Lemon and Tomatoes
From Metaftsis Restaurant, Volos.

Serves 6

6 fish cutlets, 2.5 cm (1 in) thick
    (use jewfish, snapper or any
    firm white-fleshed fish)
salt
freshly ground black pepper
juice 2 lemons
2 cups (16 fl oz) water

½ cup (4 fl oz) olive oil
2 teaspoons dried oregano
3 fresh tomatoes, peeled and
    sliced
½ cup (2 oz) dried breadcrumbs
3 sprigs parsley, finely chopped

1. Preheat the oven to 200° C (400° F/Gas 6).
2. Arrange the fish cutlets in a baking dish 5 cm (2 in) deep.
3. Combine the rest of the ingredients except the sliced tomatoes, breadcrumbs and parsley, and pour them over the fish.
4. Arrange the tomato slices on top and sprinkle with breadcrumbs and parsley.
5. Place the baking dish in the preheated oven and cook for 30 minutes. Serve hot.

Psári tis Skaras

Grilled Marinated Snapper
Serves 6

6 'plate-size' (approximately
    500-600 g) snapper or bream,
    cleaned and scaled
¼ cup (2 fl oz) olive oil
¼ cup (2 fl oz) dry white wine
1 clove garlic, crushed

4 sprigs parsley, finely chopped
3 sprigs mint, finely chopped
salt
freshly ground black pepper
juice 1 lemon

1. Place the fish in a deep baking dish.
2. Prepare the marinade by mixing the remaining ingredients, except lemon juice. Pour it over the fish and cover with plastic film.
3. Refrigerate for at least 3 hours, turning the fish occasionally.
4. Preheat the griller.
5. Drain the fish and reserve the marinade.
6. Place the fish under the griller, baste frequently with the marinade and grill for 5 to 8 minutes on each side.
7. Serve sprinkled with the pan juices and lemon juice.

Psári Marinato

Marinated Fried Fish
Serves 4

4 large fish fillets
salt
freshly ground black pepper
flour
½ cup (4 fl oz) olive oil

1 clove garlic
4 bay leaves
2 sprigs fresh rosemary, chopped
⅓ cup (2½ fl oz) wine vinegar
1½ cups (12 fl oz) water

1. Sprinkle the fish with salt and pepper and dust with flour.
2. Heat the oil and fry the fish until crisp and brown.
3. Place the fish in a glass or china dish.
4. To the oil in the pan, add garlic, bay leaves and rosemary, and sauté lightly until garlic browns.
5. Add the vinegar and water, and simmer for 20 minutes. Taste for seasoning.
6. Pour the marinade over the fish and refrigerate overnight, turning the fish occasionally.
7. Serve at room temperature with a fresh salad and crusty bread.

Psári Savori

Fish with Piquant Tomato Sauce
Serves 4

8 fillets of snapper
salt
freshly ground black pepper
½ cup (2 oz) flour
1 cup (8 fl oz) olive oil
1 onion, finely chopped
1 clove garlic, crushed

4 ripe tomatoes, peeled and
  chopped
1 tablespoon tomato purée
2 tablespoons wine vinegar
2 bay leaves
salt
freshly ground black pepper

1. Season the fish fillets, then dust them with flour. Fry them lightly in the oil in a frying pan.
2. Arrange the fried fish on a serving platter.
3. To the frying pan add the onion and garlic and sauté until the onion is soft and transparent.
4. Add the tomatoes, tomato purée, vinegar, bay leaves, salt and pepper.
6. Simmer until most of the moisture evaporates.
7. Spread the mixture over the fish, cool, and serve at room temperature with fresh crusty bread and a Greek salad.

Right: Parthenon, Acropolis, Athens.

Bakaliáros Tiganitós

Deep-fried Cod
Serves 4

1.25 kg (2½ lb) salt cod
3 cups (12 oz) self-raising flour
1¾ cups (14 fl oz) lukewarm
  water
½ teaspoon salt

oil for frying
Skordaliá sauce (see p. 36)
lemon wedges for garnish

1. Soak the cod for 12 hours before preparation and change the water several times.
2. Rinse the fish under running water and cut it into pieces 5 cm (2 in) long and 2.5 cm (1 in) wide.
3. To make the batter, put the flour in a mixing bowl and, while stirring, gradually add the water and salt. Set it aside for 1 to 2 hours.
4. Dust the pieces of fish in a little flour and then dip them in the batter.
5. Deep fry them in the hot oil until the batter is golden brown.
6. Serve hot with Skordaliá sauce and garnish with lemon wedges.

Oktapódi Krassáto

Octopus in Wine
Serves 4

1 kg (2 lb) octopus
½ cup (4 fl oz) olive oil
2 onions, finely chopped
3 stalks celery, chopped
1 clove garlic
3 bay leaves

1 tablespoon tomato paste
3 cups (24 fl oz) dry red wine
3 tomatoes, peeled and chopped
1 teaspoon salt
freshly ground black pepper

1. Octopus is already tenderised when bought. Clean by emptying out the body.
2. Rinse well under running water and cut up into bite-size pieces.
3. In a saucepan, sauté the octopus in the oil together with the onions, celery and garlic for 20 minutes.
4. Add the bay leaves, tomato paste diluted in the wine, the tomatoes, salt and pepper.
5. Cover the saucepan and simmer for 2 hours or until the octopus is tender.
6. If necessary, adjust seasoning. Serve hot.

Kalamarákia Tiganitá I

Deep-fried Squid
Serves 6

1 cup (8 fl oz) water
2 eggs
200 g (6½ oz) flour
1 cup (4 oz) dry breadcrumbs
salt
freshly ground black pepper
1 teaspoon paprika

1 clove garlic, crushed
24 small squid with tentacles, or
  6 large squid cut into pieces
1 cup (8 fl oz) frying oil
juice 2 lemons
6 lemon wedges

1. In a bowl, whisk the water and eggs.
2. In a second bowl, combine the flour, breadcrumbs, salt, pepper, paprika and garlic.
3. Dip the squid first in the egg mixture and then in the flour mixture, coating the squid evenly.
4. Heat the oil in a frying pan and fry the squid for 3 to 5 minutes until light brown.
5. Drain on kitchen paper.
6. Serve hot, sprinkled with lemon juice and garnished with lemon wedges.

Kalamarákia Tiganitá II

Fried Squid Rings
Serves 4

1 kg (2 lb) squid, cleaned and cut
  into rings 6 mm (¼ in) wide
2 cups (16 fl oz) milk
1½ cups (6 oz) flour
salt

1½ cups (12 fl oz) water
freshly ground black pepper
3 sprigs parsley, chopped
1 lemon, cut into wedges

1. To tenderise the squid, soak it in the milk for 4 to 6 hours.
2. Dry the squid. Using ½ cup (2 oz) flour, dust the squid rings thoroughly.
3. Make a batter by mixing the remaining flour, salt and enough water to make a liquid batter.
4. Dip the squid in the batter and fry them crisp and golden brown.
5. Serve hot, sprinkled with salt, pepper and parsley and garnished with lemon wedges.

Kalamaria Yemistá

Stuffed Squid
From **Costoyanis Taverna,** *Athens.*

Serves 6

12 squid, each approximately
   12 cm (5 in) long
½ cup (4 fl oz) olive oil
2 onions, finely chopped
4 sprigs parsley, finely chopped
1 cup (5 oz) cooked rice
2 tablespoons pine nuts

1 tablespoon tomato paste
¼ cup (1½ oz) currants
salt
freshly ground black pepper
1 cup (8 fl oz) dry white wine
½ cup (4 fl oz) water

1. Preheat the oven to 180° C (350° F/Gas 4).
2. Under running water, clean the squid, making sure that the sack is not cut. Chop and retain the tentacles for the stuffing.
3. In half of the oil, fry the onions until they are golden brown. Add the tentacles and cook for 5 minutes.
4. Add the parsley, cooked rice, pine nuts, tomato paste, currants, salt and pepper and cook for a further 5 minutes. Cool.
5. The stuffing will swell during cooking, so stuff the squid lightly. Secure the openings with toothpicks.
6. Pour the wine and water into a heavy-bottomed oven dish and lay the squid side by side.
7. Cover the dish with foil, and bake in the preheated oven for 1 hour or until the squid are tender. Serve hot with the cooking juices poured over the squid.

   Right: Local fisherman tenderising an octopus by beating it against the pavement.

Tonnos Souvlákia

Grilled Tuna Skewers
The original recipe was for swordfish, which is not readily available, so tuna is used here.

Serves 6

1 kg (2 lb) fresh tuna, cut into
   4 cm (1½ in) cubes
juice 3 lemons
¼ cup (2 fl oz) olive oil
3 sprigs parsley, finely chopped

2 sprigs fresh rosemary chopped
   or 1 teaspoon dried rosemary
salt
freshly ground black pepper
bay leaves, preferably fresh

1. Marinate the tuna cubes in the marinade prepared from the remaining ingredients, except bay leaves, for 1 hour.
2. Drain the fish and reserve the marinade.
3. Preheat the griller.
4. Divide the fish cubes into 4 portions and place on 4 skewers alternating with bay leaves.
5. Place the skewers under the griller and baste frequently, using up all the marinade.
6. When cooked, serve on individual plates and pour the cooking juices over the fish.

Psári Plakí

Baked Fish with Vegetables
An extravagant dish but very delicious and worth the effort.

Serves 6

12 fish fillets (2 per person)

Marinade:
juice 2 lemons
1 teaspoon salt
freshly ground black pepper
1 teaspoon oregano
2 tablespoons oil
2 ripe tomatoes, peeled and coarsely chopped
1 onion, halved and thinly sliced
2 green peppers (capsicums), seeded and thinly sliced

Vegetables:
½ cup (4 fl oz) olive oil
3 sprigs parsley, finely chopped
3 tomatoes, peeled and coarsely chopped
500 g (1 lb) fresh spinach, coarsely chopped
2 zucchini (courgettes), cut into thick slices
3 onions, thinly sliced
2 stalks celery, chopped
1 cup (8 fl oz) dry white wine
4 tablespoons tomato purée
2 teaspoons salt
freshly ground black pepper
2 lemons, thinly sliced
3 potatoes, peeled and thickly sliced

1. Put the fish in a glass or china dish.
2. Combine all ingredients of the marinade and pour them over the fish.
3. Refrigerate the fish for 4 hours.
4. Preheat the oven to 190° C (375° F/Gas 5).
5. In a large frying pan, heat the oil and add the vegetables taken from the fish marinade.
6. Add parsley, tomatoes, spinach, zucchini, onions and celery and sauté for 15 minutes.
7. Add wine, tomato purée, salt and pepper and sauté for a further 20 minutes.
8. Arrange the fish in the centre of a large baking dish. Place the vegetables around it. Place the lemon slices on top of the fish and potato slices on top of the vegetables.
9. Bake in the preheated oven for 1 hour. Serve hot, by itself as a main-course dish.

MEATS

The flat but gentle sound of bells woke me very early one morning during my visit to Delphi – a motley flock of woolly sheep was slowly passing by, while grazing what seemed almost-barren ground. Yet they look contented and well fed.

Pastures in Greece are sparse yet the lamb and kid that grow on this hardy diet are tender and sweet. Wild herbs and aromatic grass give the meat a good flavour.

Mutton and goat are not very popular. And beef, which requires solid pastures, is rare, frequently imported and not always of good quality.

Being limited in their choice, over the ages the Greeks have accepted the limitations and have developed the preparation of lamb to a fine art. Lemon juice, garlic and oregano (a herb so frequently used in Greek cooking), together with slices of onion and celery, combine to give roasted leg of lamb à la Grecque its unmistakable flavour. Souvlákia, a close relation of the Turkish Shish Kebab, its meat marinated overnight, evokes images of Greece. Moussaká, a dish originally designed to stretch what little meat was available, is today one of the most popular of typical dishes.

Braising is a popular method of cooking and I think that it brings the best flavour out in lamb; lamb shanks, braised with artichokes in an egg-lemon sauce, is among my favourite dishes.

Greek meatballs, Keftédes, done in various sauces are also popular.

Whatever Greeks do with their meat, they always manage not only to preserve the natural flavour but also, through the use of the appropriate vegetables and herbs, to enhance it and create that great 'Greek' flavour.

Amalia Hotel, Delphi

The temple complex of Delphi was one of the most important shrines of ancient Greece. As the site of the Pythian Oracle it was the place of pilgrimage for the common man as well as for the great and mighty who travelled to Delphi to seek guidance.

Today only ruins remain but the beautiful setting has remained unchanged. Like the seating of an amphitheatre, the many levels on which the ancient buildings were erected rise from the winding road. Even in their present devastated state, the ruins bear witness of the past splendour. Half way up the hill are the ruins of the temple which was dedicated to Apollo, the guardian of the oracle. The whole site stands against the majestic backdrop of Mt Kirfis which dominates the tranquil valley.

Farther down the road is the quiet town of Delphi and, just outside the township, the Amalia Hotel. Recently built, it overlooks the olive groves which descend to Itea on the Corinthian Gulf.

Like its sister hotel in Olympia, the Amalia provides all the amenities of a modern hotel. The food is mainly international but on the day of my visit there were some typical Greek dishes served: Youvétsi (the tasty lamb casserole with pasta), roast lamb, Greek salad and the famous olives from the nearby Amfissa.

Right: Lamb Casserole with Pasta (p. 85) and Seasoned Roast Leg of Lamb (p. 86).

Pipperiés ke Domátes Yemistés

Stuffed Peppers and Tomatoes
From **Restaurant Kuyu,** *Piraeus.*

This dish is very popular in Greece and can be found, at one time or another, in all Greek homes as well as in most restaurants. Not only peppers and tomatoes are prepared in this fashion but also zucchini and eggplant. It is important to note that the different vegetables require varying baking times.

Serves 4

4 large firm tomatoes	500 g (1 lb) minced beef or lamb
1 teaspoon sugar	500 g (1 lb) peeled, chopped tomatoes
4 large green peppers (capsicums)	2 tablespoons tomato paste
¾ cup (4 oz) long-grain rice	salt
4 tablespoons olive oil	freshly ground black pepper
1 onion, chopped	6 mint leaves, finely chopped
¼ bunch parsley, finely chopped	½ cup (4 fl oz) dry red wine

1. Preheat the oven to 180°C (350°F/Gas 4).
2. Cut a thin 'lid' off the top of each tomato. With a teaspoon, scoop out the pulp, chop it and set it aside for the stuffing.
3. Sprinkle the inside of the tomatoes with the sugar and place them upside down to drain.
4. Cut the top off each pepper, scoop out and discard the seeds.
5. Plunge the peppers and their lids into boiling water and cook for 5 minutes. Drain and place them into some cold water.
6. In ½ cup of water, parboil the rice.
7. In 2 tablespoons of the oil, sauté the chopped onion until it is soft and transparent, then add the parsley.
8. Add the reserved tomato pulp, the peeled and chopped tomatoes, and the tomato paste, salt and pepper, mint and wine.
9. Mix well and simmer over low heat for 20 minutes, stirring occasionally. If the mixture dries out, add some water.
10. Separately, in the remaining 2 tablespoons of oil, fry the meat until brown, stirring constantly.
11. To the meat add the parboiled rice and two-thirds of the tomato sauce.
12. On low heat, cook this stuffing for 10 minutes, stirring occasionally. If necessary add some water to keep the mixture moist. Remove from heat and cool.
13. Stand the peppers and the tomatoes in two separate baking dishes and with a teaspoon fill each loosely with some stuffing.
14. Replace the lids, pour the remaining tomato sauce into the dishes, cover them with foil and cook them in the preheated oven, the peppers for 35 minutes and the tomatoes for 15 minutes.
15. Remove the foil and cook both for a further 10 minutes basting them with the caps removed. Serve hot with the remaining tomato sauce.

Souvlákia

Lamb on Skewers
From **Restaurant Marmara,** Mistras.

Souvlákia is basically marinated meat, grilled on a skewer. The most popular meat is lamb, though beef and poultry are also used. The meat can be skewered plain or it may be skewered with tomatoes, mushrooms, onions and green peppers. At the Marmara, meat and vegetables are combined.

Serves 6

1 cup (8 fl oz) olive oil
juice 2 lemons
½ cup (4 fl oz) dry red wine
1 clove garlic, crushed
2 bay leaves
½ teaspoon salt
freshly ground black pepper

1½ tablespoons dried oregano
1.5 kg (3 lb) lamb from a leg, cut
  into 4 cm (1½ in) cubes
3 green peppers (capsicums)
2 onions, each cut into 6 wedges
12-18 small button mushrooms
3-4 tomatoes, cut into quarters

1. In a large bowl combine oil, lemon juice, wine, garlic, bay leaves, salt and pepper and oregano.
2. Mix well and add the meat.
3. Halve the green peppers (capsicums), remove and discard the seeds, cut the peppers into 2.5 cm (1 in) squares.
4. Boil some salted water and plunge in the peppers and onions. Boil them for 5 minutes. Rinse them in cold water and add them to the marinade.
5. Marinate for 24 hours.
6. Two hours before grilling the skewers, add the mushrooms and the tomatoes to the marinade.
7. Allow 1 skewer per person. Divide all the ingredients equally between the six skewers and thread a piece of lamb, pepper, onion, mushroom, tomato and then repeat.
8. At each end allow some of the skewer to project for easy turning.
9. Grill either over an open charcoal fire or under a griller for some 15 minutes until cooked to taste. While grilling, frequently baste with the marinade. Occasionally, Souvlákia is served on a bed of rice pilaf.

Keftéthes

Greek Meatballs
*From **Amalia Hotel**, Olympia.*

Yields 48 egg-sized meatballs

1 onion, finely chopped
1 tablespoon olive oil
1 kg (2 lb) finely minced lamb, beef or veal
4¼ cups (8 oz) soft breadcrumbs
2 teaspoons finely chopped mint
3 sprigs parsley, finely chopped
2 teaspoons salt

freshly ground black pepper
juice 1 lemon
2-3 tablespoons Ouzo, or ½ cup (4 fl oz) dry red wine
2 eggs lightly beaten
½ cup (2 oz) flour
⅔ cup (5 fl oz) olive oil for frying

1. Lightly fry the onion in 1 tablespoon of oil until golden.
2. Combine all ingredients except flour and the oil for frying. Knead well until the mixture is blended and smooth.
3. Shape it into balls. The size may vary, depending on whether they are to be small walnut-sized balls for cocktails or large-sized balls for a main course dish.
4. Roll the balls in flour.
5. Cook them in hot oil, rolling them until they are brown on all sides.

Right: One of the many temple sites at Delphi.

Pastitso I

Macaroni Eggplant Moussaká
From **Arvanitia Beach Restaurant**, *Nafplio*.

A Greek friend told me once that there are as many Moussakás as there are cooks in Greece. A slight exaggeration! However, as with most cooking, Greek recipes lend themselves to many variations. Moussakás are made also with potatoes, potatoes and eggplant, or with pumpkins. In all, the end result is worth the rather laborious preparation.

Serves 6-8

500 g (1 lb) eggplant (aubergine)
salt
45 g (1½ oz) flour
1 cup (4 fl oz) olive oil
300 g (about 2 cups) cooked
  macaroni

Meat Sauce:
1 onion, finely chopped
1 garlic clove, crushed
1 kg (2 lb) minced lamb
250 g (1 cup) peeled, drained,
  canned tomatoes
1 cup (4 fl oz) tomato juice from
  the canned tomatoes
2 tablespoons tomato paste
1 teaspoon dried oregano
½ teaspoon cinnamon
½ cup (4 fl oz) dry red wine
salt
freshly ground black pepper

Cream Sauce:
45 g (1½ oz) butter
½ cup (2 oz) flour
2 cups (16 fl oz) hot milk
2 eggs, lightly beaten
30 g (1 oz) Kefalotíri or
  Parmesan cheese, grated
salt
freshly ground black pepper

Topping:
30 g (1 oz) Kefalotíri of
  Parmesan cheese, grated

1. Slice the unpeeled eggplant into slices 1.5 cm (½ in) thick, sprinkle them with salt and leave them to drain for an hour.
2. Dry the slices with paper towels.
3. Dust the slices with flour and fry them in some of the oil for about 2 minutes each side.
4. Place the cooked slices on kitchen paper to drain off excess oil.

Meat Sauce:
1. In the remaining oil, lightly fry the onion and garlic.
2. Add the meat and brown it while mashing it with the back of a fork to break up the lumps.
3. Add the tomatoes, tomato juice and tomato paste, oregano, cinnamon and wine.
4. Simmer gently until enough liquid has evaporated and the sauce is thick. Season to taste.

Cream Sauce:
1. Melt the butter, add the flour and cook gently without browning for 3 minutes.
2. Stir in the hot milk, stir vigorously and cook for 2 to 3 minutes until the sauce is smooth.
3. Take off the heat, stir in the eggs and 30 g grated cheese. Season to taste.

Assembly of the Moussaká:
1. Preheat the oven to 180° C (350° F/Gas 4).
2. Grease a rectangular, glazed earthenware or glass oven dish approximately 35 x 25 x 5 cm (14 x 10 x 2 in).
3. Arrange a layer of eggplant on the bottom of the dish. Place half of the cooked macaroni on top of it and cover it with half of the meat sauce. Then add the remainder of the macaroni and the meat. Finish it with the rest of the eggplant and spread the cream sauce on top. Sprinkle it with the remaining cheese and bake it in the oven for 1 hour. If necessary, brown the top under the grill.
4. Remove from oven, let it stand for 5 to 10 minutes before serving. Cut into square portions.

Youvétsi

Lamb Casserole with Pasta
From **Hotel Amalia**, *Delphi*.

Serves 6

1½ kg (3 lb) shoulder of lamb, cut into 6 pieces
½ cup (4 fl oz) oil
1 onion, finely chopped
1 garlic clove, chopped
6 ripe tomatoes, peeled and chopped
1 teaspoon dried oregano

salt
freshly ground black pepper
6 cups (1.5 litres) boiling water
500 g (1 lb) minestra (rice-shaped pasta, also called Orzo)
150 g (5 oz) grated Kefalotíri or Parmesan cheese

1. Preheat the oven to 180°C (350°F /Gas 4).
2. In a casserole on top of the stove, brown the pieces of meat in the oil.
3. Add the onion and garlic and cook until the onion is soft and transparent.
4. Add the tomatoes and oregano and season with salt and pepper.
5. Cover the casserole and cook in the preheated oven for 1 hour.
6. Add the boiling water and the minestra.
7. Cover and return to the oven for a further 30 minutes, stirring occasionally.
8. Serve directly out of the casserole and sprinkle with the grated cheese.

Arní Psito

Seasoned Roast Leg of Lamb
Serves 6-8

3-3.5 kg (6-7 lb) leg of lamb
2 garlic cloves, cut into small slivers
1 teaspoon dried oregano
1 teaspoon grated lemon peel

salt
freshly ground black pepper
juice 3-4 lemons
1 cup (8 fl oz) dry white wine

1. Preheat the oven to 180°C (350°F/Gas 4).
2. Trim off most of the fat leaving the membrane covering the meat.
3. In a bowl, combine the garlic slivers, oregano, lemon peel, salt and pepper.
4. With a sharp knife, make incisions 2.5 cm (1 in) deep on all sides of the leg, and into them insert the garlic slivers together with some of the oregano-peel-salt-pepper mixture.
5. Place the lamb in a baking dish, rub it with some lemon juice and season it with salt and pepper.
6. Roast it in the oven for 1½ hours. Combine the lemon juice and the white wine and occasionally baste the leg.
7. When cooked, let it stand for 10 minutes. This will stop the flow of juices and make the carving easier. Taste, and if necessary season the cooking juices and pour some over each serving.

Hotel Divani, Kalambaka

At Meteora nature and man have teamed up to create one of the most fascinating places which, in a country that abounds with countless interesting attractions, is quite a feat.

Meteora is an unusual phenomenon of nature. Twenty-four cyclopean rocks rise vertically to the sky. Partly polished smooth by the ages, partly pitted with caves and crevises, they present an awe-inspiring sight. It is their appearance that must have impressed ancient hermits who chose them as shelter.

The presence of the hermits as well as the mysterious appearance of the rocks attracted worshippers and by the 14th century it is recorded that a number of monasteries were built, perched on the pinnacles of the rocks. At the height of their development there were twenty-four monasteries flourishing in the area. However, because of their strategic position, over the ages most have been subject to fire and sword. Today only four of the largest are still inhabited by monks. And despite the destruction, many fine examples of Byzantine art have survived.

The township of Kalambaka is the basis from which to visit Meteora. Against the backdrop of the rocks, the Hotel Divani offers modern comfort for the weary traveller, which is in contrast to the monastic simplicity that exists a few kilometres away. Simple, tasty Greek food supplements the international cuisine offered at the hotel.

Right: Top to bottom: Souvalki (p. 81); Greek Salad (p. 42); Rice-stuffed vine leaves (p. 12).

Arni me Angináres Avgolémono

Lamb Shanks and Artichokes with Egg-lemon Sauce

*From **Gerofinikas**, Athens.*

Serves 6

6 large or 12 small artichokes	**2 stalks celery, chopped**
½ cup (2 oz) cornflour (cornstarch)	**1 onion, chopped**
salt	**3 eggs, separated**
juice and rind of 2 lemons	**salt**
12 small lamb shanks	**juice 3 lemons**
12 peppercorns	**freshly ground black pepper**
4 bay leaves	**3 sprigs parsley, finely chopped**
1 carrot, chopped	

1. Wash the artichokes and trim each by breaking off all coarse outer leaves.
2. Cut the stalk at a point where it breaks easily. Leave the remainder of the stalk on the artichoke as it will be tender and edible.
3. Lay the artichoke on its side and cut 2.5-4 cm (1-1½ in) off the tips of the leaves.
4. Dissolve the cornflour in 4 cups (1 litre) of water, add the lemon juice and the rind and place the artichokes in this as soon as they are trimmed. This will prevent discolouration.
5. Strain the artichokes and put the liquid into a large saucepan. Add enough fresh water to cover the artichokes and bring to the boil. Add the artichokes, cover them with a teatowel and place a lid on the pan.
6. Boil for 15 to 25 minutes depending on their size. Remove with slotted spoon, gently part the leaves and remove and discard the choke. Keep them warm.
7. To cook the lamb shanks, in a saucepan with enough water to cover the shanks add salt, peppercorns, bay leaves, carrot, celery and onion. On low heat, simmer the lamb shanks for 1½ hours. Take off the heat and let them stand until the sauce is prepared. (1½ cups of the stock will be used in step 11.)
8. To prepare egg and lemon sauce, beat the egg whites with a pinch of salt until stiff.
9. Continue beating and add the egg yolks and the juice of 3 lemons.
10. While beating continuously, add 1½ cups (12 fl oz) of the hot lamb stock to the egg-lemon mixture.
11. Heat for 2 to 3 minutes until the sauce thickens but do not boil. Season to taste.
12. To serve, arrange the hot lamb shanks and artichokes on a serving dish, pour the sauce over and garnish with the parsley. Serve immediately.

Arní Psito sto Chanti

Lamb Chops in Filo Pastry

This is an adaptation of a dish which originally required the chops to be baked 'en papillotes' (wrapped in paper).

Serves 6

6 lamb leg chops
¼ cup (2 fl oz) olive oil
3 onions, chopped
1 clove garlic, crushed
4 ripe fresh tomatoes, peeled and chopped
2 teaspoons dried thyme
2 teaspoons dried oregano
2 teaspoons dried basil

2 teaspoons fresh mint leaves, chopped
salt
freshly ground black pepper
juice 3 lemons
6 slices Kasséri or Swiss cheese
12 sheets filo pastry
½ cup (4 oz) melted butter

1. Preheat the oven to 200° C (400° F/Gas 6).
2. Lightly fry the chops in the oil for 5 minutes. Remove from the pan and set aside.
3. In the same pan in oil, fry the onions and garlic until the onions are transparent and soft.
4. Add the tomatoes, herbs, salt, pepper and lemon juice and simmer until all liquid has evaporated.
5. Using two sheets of filo pastry per chop, put down first one sheet, coat it generously with melted butter, then place a second sheet on top. Place the chop on this, at one end of the pastry rectangle. On top of the chop spoon one-sixth of the mixture and cover it with a slice of cheese.
   To wrap the chop, first fold the two sides of the filo inwards over the chop, then fold the end of the sheet over the meat and roll it around the chop.
6. Brush with melted butter all around. Place the wrapped chops on a buttered baking dish.
7. Bake in the preheated oven for 30 minutes or until golden brown.

Arní Fricassée me Maroúlia

Lamb Fricassée with Lettuce
From Costoyanis Taverna, Athens

Serves 6

1.25 kg (2½ lb) breast of
    shoulder of lamb, cut into
    2.5 cm (1 in) cubes
2 onions, sliced
6 spring onions (scallions), sliced
125 g (4 oz) butter
2 tablespoons flour
2 small lettuces, shredded
4 cups (1 litre) water

1 tablespoon salt
freshly ground black pepper
4 sprigs parsley, chopped
3 sprigs dill, chopped
3 egg yolks
2 tablespoons water
juice 1½-2 lemons

1. Sauté the meat, onions and spring onions in the butter for 5 minutes.
2. Sprinkle with flour and, while stirring, fry for 2 minutes.
3. Add the lettuce, water, salt, pepper, parsley and dill.
4. Simmer covered for 1 hour. Remove from heat.
5. Beat the egg yolks, water and lemon juice together. Continue beating and add ¼ cup (2 fl oz) of the lamb cooking juice.
6. Return the lamb to the heat and while stirring constantly add the egg mixture to the juices. Do not boil. Serve hot.

Right: Ancient olive trees, Sparta.

Arní Bóuti tou Fóurnou me Patátes

Roast Leg of Lamb Greek Style, with Potatoes
The lamb in the recipe is roasted and partly braised for a long time which gives it the characteristic succulent texture and flavour.

Serves 6

3 kg (7 lb) leg of lamb
juice 2 lemons
salt
freshly ground black pepper
3 tablespoons dried oregano
1 clove garlic, cut into slivers

1 cup (8 fl oz) dry white wine or water
1 onion, sliced
1 stalk celery, chopped
6 large potatoes, peeled and cut into quarters

1. Preheat the oven to 200°C (400°F/Gas 6).
2. Rub the leg of lamb with half of the lemon juice. Sprinkle it with salt, pepper and some of the oregano.
3. With a sharp knife, make deep cuts in the leg and insert the garlic slivers.
4. Place the meat, fat side up, in a baking dish without lid. Cook in the preheated oven for 1 hour.
5. Add the wine or water (or a mixture of both), the onion and the celery. Turn down the heat to 160°C (325°F/Gas 3) and cook for 2 hours. Check occasionally and add more wine or water if necessary.
6. Add the potatoes to the pan, sprinkle them with the remaining lemon juice, salt, pepper and oregano.
7. Continue roasting for 20 minutes. Turn the potatoes and roast for another 30 minutes or until potatoes are brown and cooked.
8. To serve, cut the meat into chunks, place them on a serving platter and arrange the potatoes around it. Skim the fat off the cooking juices, season and pour it over the meat and potatoes.

Arní me Bámies

Lamb Stew with Okra
Serves 4-6

500 g (16 oz) okra (ladies'
    fingers), washed and trimmed
¼ cup (2 fl oz) vinegar
750 g (1½ lb) lean shoulder of
    lamb, cut into 2.5 cm (1 in)
    cubes
1 onion, finely chopped

2 tablespoons olive oil
45 g (1½ oz) butter
1 tablespoon tomato paste
water
salt
freshly ground black pepper

1. Place the okra in a bowl, pour the vinegar over it and let it marinate for
   30 minutes.
2. Brown the meat and onions in the olive oil and butter.
3. Add tomato paste and enough water to cover the meat. Season.
4. Cover and simmer over low heat for 1½ hours.
5. In the meantime, take the okra out of the marinade and rinse off the
   vinegar.
6. Put the okra in a saucepan and ladle a little of the cooking liquid off the
   meat into the saucepan. Cover and simmer for 15 to 20 minutes.
7. Place the meat in the centre of a serving plate and arrange the okra
   neatly around it. Pour over the sauce and serve hot.

Fasoulákia me Kréas

Braised Lamb with Beans
Serves 4-6

1 kg (2 lb) shoulder of lamb, cut
    into 2.5 cm (1 in) cubes
3 tablespoons flour
⅓ cup (2½ fl oz) olive oil
salt
freshly ground black pepper
2 onions, finely chopped

1 clove garlic, crushed
1 cup (8 fl oz) dry white wine
4 tomatoes, peeled and chopped
2 tablespoons tomato paste
¼ teaspoon cinnamon
1 kg (2 lb) fresh green beans,
    trimmed, cut in half and
    parboiled

1. Coat the meat cubes in flour.
2. Heat 3 tablespoons of the oil in a lidded casserole and brown the meat on
   all sides. Season.
3. In a frying pan, heat the rest of the oil and sauté the onions and garlic
   until the onions are soft and transparent.
4. To the onion-garlic mixture add wine, tomatoes, tomato paste and
   cinnamon, simmer for 10 minutes.
5. Add to the meat, cover the casserole and simmer over low heat for 1
   hour.
6. Add the parboiled beans and simmer for a further 15 minutes. Serve hot
   with a Greek salad.

Arní me Kithonia

Lamb with Quinces
Serves 4-6

1 kg (2 lb) shoulder of lamb, cut
  into 2 cm (1 in) cubes
3 tablespoons flour
5 tablespoons (3 fl oz) olive oil
salt
freshly ground black pepper
2 onions, finely chopped
3 tomatoes, peeled and chopped

2 tablespoons tomato paste
1 teaspoon sugar or honey
1 cup (8 fl oz) dry white wine or
  water
juice ½ lemon
1 kg (2 lb) quinces, peeled,
  quartered and sliced

1. Dust the meat with flour.
2. In a casserole, heat 3 tablespoons of the olive oil and brown the meat all round. Season.
3. Add onions and sauté until the onions are soft and transparent.
4. Add tomatoes, tomato paste, sugar or honey, wine and lemon juice, cover and simmer over low heat for 1¼ hours.
5. Add the quinces and if necessary some water. Continue cooking for a further 30 minutes. Season to taste and serve hot with mashed potatoes.

Right: A colourful street in Corfu.

Spengiofai

Sausages with Green Peppers, Onions and Tomatoes
*From **Pileas Restaurant**, Hania, Mt Pelion.*

Spengiofai is a delicious local speciality and although I was not able to get the recipe for the particular sausages used the following is an adaptation which is equally tasty.

Makes 36 main-course sausages
Serves 6-8

Sausages:
750 g (1½ lb) coarsely minced
  pork
250 g (8 oz) coarsely minced beef
1 teaspoon salt
12 peppercorns, cracked
1 garlic clove, crushed
1 teaspoon cinnamon
2 teaspoons chopped savoury
1 teaspoon allspice
grated rind of 1 orange
½ cup (4 fl oz) dry red wine

Sauce:
2 green peppers (capsicums),
  seeded and cut in slices
4 onions, chopped
¼ cup (2 fl oz) olive oil
4 tomatoes, peeled and chopped
2 tablespoons tomato paste
1 cup (8 fl oz) water
1 cup (8 fl oz) dry white wine
1 teaspoon oregano
salt
freshly ground black pepper

1. Mix all the sausage ingredients and refrigerate for 12 hours.
2. Fry the green peppers (capsicums) and the onions in the oil for 5 to 8 minutes.
3. Add the tomatoes, tomato paste, water, wine, oregano and seasoning.
4. Cook for 5 minutes.
5. Form the meat mixture into 36 sausage-shaped cylinders or meatballs.
6. Fry them until brown.
7. In a casserole combine sausages and sauce, cover with a lid and casserole for 30 minutes.

Prassópitta

Leek and Meat Pie
Serves 8

Cream Sauce:
60 g (2 oz) butter
90 g (3 oz) flour
3 cups (24 fl oz) hot milk
3 eggs, lightly beaten
45 g (1½ oz) Kefalotíri or
 Parmesan cheese, grated
salt
freshly ground black pepper

1 kg (2 lb) leeks, use bulbs and
 white part of leaves only,
 finely chopped
1½ cups (12 oz) melted unsalted
 butter
500 g (1 lb) minced lamb or a
 mixture of minced veal and
 pork
¼ cup (2 fl oz) dry white wine
salt
freshly ground black pepper
¼ teaspoon nutmeg
375 g (12 oz) filo pastry

1. Prepare the cream sauce first. Melt the butter, add the flour and cook gently without browning for 3 minutes.
2. Stir in the hot milk, stir vigorously and cook for 2 to 3 minutes until the sauce is smooth.
3. Take off the heat, stir in the eggs and the cheese. Season to taste.
4. Preheat the oven to 180°C (350° F/Gas 4).
5. Sauté the leeks in 1½ tablespoons of melted butter until soft. Remove from pan and set aside.
6. In some more butter, fry the minced meat for 15 minutes, mashing it with a fork.
7. Add the wine, salt and pepper and nutmeg. Simmer until most of the wine has evaporated.
8. In a large bowl, combine the leeks, meat and cream sauce. Season to taste.
9. Grease a large baking dish approximately 50 x 35 x 5 cm (20 x 14 x 2 in) with some melted butter.
10. On the bottom and up the sides of the dish, place 8 sheets of filo pastry, each sheet generously brushed with melted butter before the next is placed.
11. Spoon and spread the mixture evenly in the pan.
12. Cover it with 10 sheets of filo pastry, each in turn, as well as the top, well brushed with melted butter.
13. Tuck the edges of the covering filo sheets around the inside edges of the pan.
14. Bake in the preheated oven for 45 minutes until golden and crisp. Cool for a few minutes and serve hot, cut into squares.

Stifátho I

Beef Stew with Onions and Red Wine
Serves 4

½ cup (4 fl oz) olive oil
1 onion, chopped
1 clove garlic, crushed
750 g (1½ lb) shin beef, cut into
    2.5 cm (1 in) cubes
4 ripe tomatoes, peeled and
    chopped
2 tablespoons tomato paste
1½ cups (12 fl oz) dry red wine
1 tablespoon red wine vinegar

water
2 bay leaves
⅛ teaspoon cumin
⅛ teaspoon cinnamon
salt
freshly ground black pepper
12-16 small (pickling-type)
    onions

1. In a heavy-bottomed casserole, heat three-quarters of the oil and fry the onions, garlic and meat until the meat is brown on all sides.
2. Add the tomatoes, tomato paste, wine and vinegar, and enough water to cover the meat.
3. Add the rest of the ingredients, except the onions.
4. Cover the casserole, bring to the boil. Reduce heat and simmer for 1½ hours.
5. In a frying pan, brown the onions in the remainder of the oil.
6. Add them to the meat and continue simmering for a further 30 to 45 minutes.
7. Before serving, season to taste. Serve hot with rice pilaf (see p. 53).

Right: Wine making in the village of Lakones on Corfu.

Stifátho II

Greek Beef and Onion Stew
Serves 6

1 kg (2 lb) shin beef, cut into
  large cubes
½ cup (4 fl oz) olive oil
1.5 kg (3 lb) small onions
3 cloves garlic, crushed

1¼ cups (10 fl oz) tomato purée
1 tablespoon dried oregano
1 cup (8 fl oz) dry red wine
salt
freshly ground black pepper

1. In a heavy-bottomed casserole, brown the meat in the oil together with the onions and garlic.
2. Add the tomato purée, oregano, wine, salt and pepper.
3. Cover, bring to the boil, reduce heat to the minimum and simmer for 3 to 4 hours until the meat is very tender and the liquid is the consistency of jam. Serve with chunky fresh bread and lots of retsina.

Kréas me Melitzanes

Braised Beef and Eggplant
Serves 4-6

1 kg (2 lb) eggplant (aubergine),
  cut into 5 cm (2 in) cubes
salt
¾ cup (6 fl oz) olive oil
1 kg (2 lb) shin beef, cut into
  5 cm (2 in) cubes
freshly ground black pepper
3 onions, chopped

1 clove garlic, crushed
5 tomatoes, peeled and chopped
2 tablespoons tomato purée
1-2 cups (8-16 fl oz) dry red wine
  or water
½ cup (2 oz) flour

1. Sprinkle the eggplant cubes with salt and place them in a colander. Cover them with a weighed-down plate for 30 minutes.
2. Heat 2 tablespoons of the oil in a saucepan or casserole and brown the meat on all sides. Season.
3. In a frying pan, heat 2 tablespoons of oil and sauté the onions and garlic until onions are golden brown.
4. Add the sautéed onions and garlic and the tomatoes, tomato purée and wine or water to the meat, cover the casserole and simmer over low heat for 1 hour.
5. Remove the eggplant from the colander, dry with paper towelling, dust with flour and fry in the remaining oil until light brown.
6. Add them to the meat and simmer for a further 30 minutes. Serve hot.

MEATS

Kreatopites

Meat Turnovers
Makes 12 turnovers

60 g (2 oz) butter
1 onion, finely chopped
1-2 cloves garlic, crushed
500 g (1 lb) minced beef
1 cup (6½ oz) tomato purée
1 cup (8 fl oz) dry red wine
salt
2 sprigs dill, chopped

½ teaspoon allspice
3 eggs, hard-boiled and finely
  chopped

Pastry:
2 cups (8 oz) flour
2½ teaspoons baking powder
100 g (3½ oz) margarine
¾ cup (6 fl oz) milk
1 egg, beaten

1. Preheat the oven to 200° C (400° F/Gas 6).
2. In a large frying pan, melt the butter and sauté the onion and garlic until the onion is soft and transparent.
3. Add the meat and with the back of a fork mash the meat to break up all lumps. Cook for 15 minutes until meat starts to brown.
4. Add the tomato purée, wine, salt, dill and allspice, and mix well. Cover the pan and cook over low heat for 40 minutes. If the meat is too dry add more wine.
5. When it is cooked, set aside and when cool, add the chopped egg.
6. To make the pastry, in a bowl mix flour, baking powder and 1 teaspoon of salt. Add margarine and mix it well. Slowly stir in the milk, do not make the dough too sticky. Rest it for 5 minutes.
6. Roll out thinly on a floured board. Cut into 12 cm (4¾ in) squares (or smaller if required for a first course).
7. Place a tablespoon of meat on each square. With a pastry brush, moisten the edge with beaten egg and fold it into a triangle. Press the edges to seal.
8. Brush the outside of each turnover with the egg. With a sharp knife, make a small slash in the top.
9. Place them on a buttered baking tray and bake in the preheated oven for 30 minutes or until golden. Serve with a salad or cooked vegetables.

101

Kréas Lemonato

Braised Beef with Lemon
Serves 4

1 kg (2 lb) shin beef, cut into small 2 cm (1 in) slices
3 tablespoons flour
3 tablespoons olive oil
3 small onions, cut into quarters
1 teaspoon dried oregano

salt
freshly ground black pepper
1 cup (8 fl oz) dry white wine
juice 1-2 lemons (according to taste)

1. Roll the meat slices in the flour.
2. In a casserole, heat the oil and fry the meat until brown.
3. Add the rest of ingredients, cover and simmer over low heat for 1½ to 2 hours until the meat is tender. Serve hot with boiled potatoes.

Marmara Restaurant, Mistras

Today in Sparta there is little indication of its past glory, of the days when Spartan warriors were the terror of ancient battlefields. The ravages of time have left few traces of the temples and shrines which formed the focal point of the Spartan settlements grouped around it on the six gentle hills that rise out of the plain of Lakonia.

Not far from modern Sparta, overlooking the plain, are the impressive foothills of Mt Taigeto. Here rise the ruins of the mediaeval Byzantine city of Mystra.

The Marmara restaurant is situated at the very bottom of that unusual hill, where ruined churches, monasteries, palaces and dwellings bear witness of a glorious past. Marmara is a good place to rest before attempting a sightseeing tour of this unusual outdoor museum of one of the last outposts of the Byzantine Empire.

The restaurant, as eating places go, has a long history. Started by the great-grandfather of the present owner more than 100 years ago, it has always served modest local Greek food. As a roadside inn it has attracted the weary traveller. And today, as in the past, the tourist stops to enjoy local stewed lamb dishes, tangy Greek salads and the local rosé wine, light in colour and refreshing to drink.

After the good meal at the Marmara, the traveller continues to the gates of Mystra, only a few minutes by road, which gives access to a unique glimpse into the past.

The castle which dominates the steep hill was built in the 13th century and around it, set in among olive groves, are the ruins of the Lower and Upper towns. During the Byzantine period many monasteries and chapels were built, and it is said that the last Byzantine emperor was crowned in the cathedral. Ruins, as well as some of the buildings still preserved, shelter fine sculptures, mosaics and frescoes of the Byzantine style.

The whole mountainside has great beauty. Orange blossoms, almond trees in full bloom and the many colourful wild flowers underfoot transform the mountain and its ruins into an enchanted garden. Every season paints a different picture.

I was there in late autumn. Muted greys, olive greens, the dark soil and the faded terracotta colour of the ruins, combined into a peaceful yet mysterious canvas.

Right: Clockwise from bottom: Lamb on Skewers (p. 81); Lamb Chops; Greek Salad (p. 42); Rice-stuffed vine leaves (p. 12).

Souzoukákia apo tin Smyŕnie

Home-made Smyrna Sausages in Tomato Sauce
Serves 6

Tomato Sauce:
2 tablespoons olive oil
2 onions, finely chopped
1.5 kg (3 lb) fresh ripe tomatoes,
    peeled and chopped
185 g (6 oz) tomato paste
4 basil leaves, chopped
1 clove garlic, crushed
1 bay leaf
½ teaspoon salt
6 peppercorns
1 tablespoon honey

Sausages:
500 g (1 lb) minced beef
½ cup (2 oz) dry breadcrumbs
1 teaspoon salt
½ teaspoon powdered cumin
¼ teaspoon cinnamon
1 clove garlic, crushed
90 g (3 oz) butter

1. In a large saucepan, heat the oil and sauté the onions until soft and transparent.
2. Add the other ingredients, cover, bring to the boil. Reduce heat and simmer for 1 hour.
3. To make the sausages, in a bowl mix meat, breadcrumbs, salt, cumin, cinnamon and garlic. Knead for 10 minutes until the mixture is the consistancy of paste. This can be done in a food processor, one cupful at a time, approximately 20-30 seconds each load.
4. Shape the mixture into small sausages 12 cm (4¾ in) long.
5. In a frying pan, heat the butter and brown the sausages.
6. Place them in a casserole, cover with tomato sauce, cover and simmer for 30 minutes. Serve with rice or pasta (sprinkled with grated cheese), and a dry red wine.

Pastítso II

Baked Macaroni and Meat
Serves 6-8

250 g (8 oz) macaroni
1 tablespoon olive oil

Meat filling:
30 g (1 oz) butter
1 large onion, finely chopped
750 g (1½ lb) minced beef
2 tablespoons tomato paste
¾ cup (6 fl oz) dry red wine
½ teaspoon nutmeg
salt
freshly ground black pepper

¼ teaspoon cinnamon
¼-½ cup (1-2 oz) dried
 breadcrumbs
1½ cups (6 oz) grated Kefalotíri
 or Parmesan cheese

Cream sauce:
4 cups milk
155 g (5 oz) butter
⅓ cup (1½ oz) flour
¼ teaspoon nutmeg
3 eggs, lightly beaten
salt

1. Preheat the oven to 180° C (350° F/Gas 4).
2. In a saucepan, cook the macaroni in boiling water with the oil until it is soft.
3. Drain and set aside.
4. To prepare the meat filling, melt the butter in a large frying pan and sauté the onion until soft and transparent.
5. Add the meat and mash it with a fork until all lumps are broken up. Cook until meat is browned.
6. Mix the tomato paste with the wine and add this to the meat. Continue cooking, add nutmeg, salt, pepper, and cinnamon.
7. Cook for about 1 hour, stirring occasionally. If the mixture is too dry, add more wine.
8. Take off the heat, cool and mix in half the breadcrumbs and half the grated cheese. Set aside.
9. To make the cream sauce, bring the milk to the boil and set aside.
10. In a saucepan, melt 125 g (4 oz) of the butter and stir in the flour. Cook over medium heat for 5 minutes.
11. Take off the heat and, while whisking vigorously, gradually add the hot milk. Keep stirring and cooking over low heat until the sauce thickens and is smooth.
12. Remove from heat and when cooled slightly, stir in the egg yolks and ¼ cup (1 oz) of the reserved cheese.
13. To assemble, grease a baking dish about 30 x 20 x 5 cm (12 x 8 x 2 in) and sprinkle it with 2 tablespoons of breadcrumbs.
14. Spread half the cooked pasta over the bottom of the dish and sprinkle it with ¼ cup (1 oz) of the reserved cheese. Spread all the meat over the pasta.
15. Pour half the sauce over the meat and spread the rest of the pasta over it. Sprinkle it with 2 tablespoons of cheese.
16. Pour the rest of the sauce on top and smooth it with a spatula.
17. Sprinkle with the rest of the cheese and breadcrumbs, dot with the remaining butter, and bake in the preheated oven for 50 to 60 minutes.
18. Take it out of the oven, let it stand for 10 minutes, cut into squares, and serve with a Greek salad and lots of chilled retsina.

Hirinó me Séllino Avgolémono

Braised Pork and Celery with Egg-lemon Sauce
Serves 4

1 kg (2 lb) lean pork, cut into
  2.5 cm (1 in) cubes
salt
freshly ground black pepper
½ cup (4 fl oz) olive oil
3 onions, finely chopped

1 cup (8 fl oz) dry white wine
2 cups (16 fl oz) water
1 head of celery, cut into 5 cm
  (2 in) lengths
2 eggs, separated
juice 1-1½ lemons

1. Season the meat and fry it in oil in a heavy-bottomed casserole, if necessary in 2 or 3 batches. Remove the fried meat and set aside.
2. In the same oil, fry the onions until soft and transparent.
3. Add the wine and water and return the meat. Cover and simmer for 45 minutes.
4. Add the celery and continue cooking for a further 15 minutes.
5. Lightly beat the egg yolks.
6. In a separate bowl, whip the egg whites with some salt until stiff, add the yolks and continue whipping to combine.
7. Take a cup of the warm cooking juice out of the casserole and add it to the eggs. Also add the lemon juice.
8. While stirring constantly add the egg mixture to the meat.
9. Heat until thick but do not boil. Season to taste. Serve hot, with a plain rice pilaf (see p. 53).

Right: The sanctuary of Pronaia Athena, Delphi.

Sikotákia me Krassi

Calf's Liver with Onions in Wine Sauce
Serves 4

500 g (1 lb) calf's or lamb's liver,
   thinly sliced (ask the butcher
   to slice it for you)
½ cup (4 fl oz) dry red wine
salt
freshly ground black pepper

30 g (1 oz) flour
¼ cup (2 fl oz) olive oil
3 onions, finely sliced
1½ cups (12 fl oz) boiling water
½ teaspoon oregano

1. Marinate the liver in the wine for 2 hours.
2. Remove the liver, sprinkle the pieces with salt and pepper and dust with flour.
3. In the oil, fry the liver for 3 to 5 minutes, depending on thickness. The liver must not be overcooked as it may become tough.
4. Set the liver aside.
5. To the frying pan, add the onions and sauté until soft and transparent.
6. Add the wine marinade, boiling water and oregano, and cook for 5 minutes. Check seasoning.
7. Add the liver to the pan for long enough for it to heat but not to cook. Serve as first course with toast or as a main course with mashed potatoes and vegetables.

Sfougato

Minced Meat and Zucchini Casserole
Serves 4

3 tablespoons olive oil
1 clove garlic, crushed
2 onions, finely chopped
500 g (1 lb) minced beef
500 g (1 lb) zucchini (courgettes),
   sliced
3 sprigs parsley, chopped

1 teaspoon dry oregano
salt
freshly ground black pepper
4 eggs, lightly beaten
½ cup (2 oz) dry breadcrumbs
45 g (1½ oz) butter

1. Preheat the oven to 180° C (350° F/Gas 4).
2. Heat the oil in a saucepan and sauté the onions, garlic, meat, zucchini, parsley, oregano and salt and pepper for 15 minutes.
3. Add the eggs and mix in well.
4. Oil a casserole and sprinkle with some of the breadcrumbs.
5. Put the mixture into the casserole, sprinkle the top with the remaining breadcrumbs, dot with butter and bake in the preheated oven for 20 to 30 minutes.

Moussaka

Serves 4

2 egg yolks, beaten
1 cup (8 fl oz) milk
salt
freshly ground pepper
1 small onion, sliced

½ cup (4 fl oz) olive oil
4 eggplant (aubergine), sliced
500 g (1 lb) cooked lamb from
  the leg, minced
½ cup (4 fl oz) beef stock (p. 141)
½ cup (4 fl oz) tomato sauce (p. 34)

1. Preheat the oven to 180° C (350° F/Gas 4).
2. Combine the egg yolks, milk, salt and pepper and cook over low heat, stirring constantly until it is like a thick custard. Set aside to cool.
3. Sauté the onion in 1 tablespoon of the oil until golden brown.
4. Lightly fry the eggplant slices in the remaining oil.
5. Oil the bottom and sides of a casserole 16 cm (6½ in) in diameter and 5 cm (2 in) deep.
6. Cover the bottom with a layer of eggplant and place some of the minced meat and fried onions on top. Repeat the layers until the ingredients are used.
7. Pour the beef stock and tomato sauce on top and cover with the custard.
8. Place the dish in the oven and bake for at least 1 hour until the top has formed a golden-brown crust. This dish may be served hot or cold.

POULTRY

Everywhere you go in the Greek countryside there are chickens. They run around the farmhouse or scratch for a meal in the shade of an olive grove. Running freely and feeding on whatever happens to be around gives them a good flavour.

While chickens are not as popular as lamb and fish, there is hardly a menu that does not feature at least one chicken dish. One of the best I tasted while in Greece was in Volos, the port of the Argonauts, in the country of the Centaurs and I was attracted by the strong and savoury aroma which permeated the air and which was emerging from a small shop where rows of chickens were rotating over a glowing fire of charcoal. Sprinkled with oregano and crisp brown on the outside, their juicy flesh was the best I had ever eaten. Washed down with lots of chilled Demestica wine, it was a meal for the gods.

In general I like what the Greek cooks do with their chicken. The basically bland flavour of chicken lends itself to a spicy and strong tasting preparation. Spices are not used extensively in Greek cooking, and chicken cooked with spices and sprinkled with grated Kefalotíri cheese is a very unusual yet tasty combination of flavours.

There is, of course, the inevitable chicken wrapped in filo pastry.

The Greeks make hearty stews and their chicken casseroles are no exception.

Whichever way they prepare them, Greeks like their chicken meat well cooked and falling off the bone, so if you like to achieve the true character, you may have to cook it more than you would normally prefer.

Gerofinikas, Athens

Gerofinikas is an old, elegant and fashionable restaurant. The present owner has been running it since 1967 and during that time its reputation for serving true Greek dishes has grown to the extent that a meal there is a must when visiting Athens.

The Greek principle of showing the dishes that are offered is strictly observed. The guests are first taken to a long counter where the food is displayed in a most appetising and tempting manner. It is difficult to resist trying all of them.

Among those I tried was lamb with artichokes with the famous Greek egg-lemon sauce. A seasonal dish prepared when the artichokes are available, it incorporates three of the best-loved ingredients: succulent lamb shanks, cooked as only the Greeks know how to prepare them, light-coloured and tender-tasting artichokes which have been specially treated so as not to discolour, and the two served with Avgolémono, the best known of Greek sauces.

Fresh swordfish with prawns wrapped in bacon and barbecued on a skewer was an unusual combination which, served with the inevitable Greek salad, was an original dish.

Gerofinikas are proud of their good Greek cuisine even if some of the dishes are of Turkish origin.

Right: Clockwise from bottom left: Lamb Shanks with Artichokes and Egg-lemon sauce (p. 88); Swordfish and prawns wrapped in bacon on skewers; Greek Salad (p. 42); Moussak (p. 109) and stuffed eggplant (in centre foreground).

Kotopoulo Riganato tis Skáras

Grilled Chicken Breasts Oregano
Serves 4

6 chicken breasts
½ cup (4 fl oz) olive oil
juice 2 lemons
2 tablespoons dried oregano or
** 3 tablespoons fresh oregano,**
** chopped**

1 tablespoon dried thyme or
** 2 tablespoons fresh thyme,**
** chopped**
salt
freshly ground black pepper

1. Place the chicken breasts in a baking dish.
2. To prepare the marinade, combine the remaining ingredients in a screw-top jar and shake well.
3. Pour the marinade over the chicken breasts and refrigerate overnight.
4. Preheat the griller and place the dish containing the chicken and the marinade under the grill.
5. Baste frequently and grill the breasts 5 minutes each side. If they are grilled too long they will be tough and dry.
6. Serve hot on a platter together with the remaining marinade.

Kota Sousámi

Fried Chicken Pieces in Sesame Batter
Serves 4

8 chicken pieces, such as breast,
** legs, thighs**
juice 2 lemons
1 teaspoon dried oregano
salt
freshly ground black pepper
1 egg, lightly beaten
½ cup (2 oz) flour

1 teaspoon almond essence
salt
freshly ground black pepper
¼ teaspoon baking powder
150 g (4½ oz) sesame seeds
oil for frying
8 sprigs parsley for garnish

1. Sprinkle the chicken pieces with lemon juice, oregano, salt and pepper and set aside for 1 hour.
2. To make the batter, combine egg, flour, almond essence, salt, pepper and baking powder. Mix to a smooth batter.
3. Dip the chicken pieces in the batter, sprinkle them with sesame seeds and some flour.
4. Heat the oil in a frying pan or deep fryer and cook the pieces until golden brown, about 5 minutes.
5. Drain on paper towels and serve hot, garnished with parsley.

Bourekakia Kotopoulo

Chicken Pie in Filo Pastry
Serves 8

100 g (3½ oz) butter
3 onions, chopped
3 stalks celery, chopped
1 clove garlic, crushed
1 kg (2 lb) coarsely chopped raw
  chicken meat
½ cup (2 oz) flour
2 cups (16 fl oz) hot chicken
  stock (see p. 140)

6 eggs, whisked
4 sprigs parsley, chopped
4 sprigs dill, chopped
juice 2 lemons
⅛ teaspoon nutmeg
salt
freshly ground black pepper
½ cup (4 oz) melted butter
12 sheets filo pastry

1. Preheat the oven to 200°C (400°F/Gas 6).
2. Heat the butter in a large frying pan and sauté the onion, celery and garlic for 5 minutes.
3. Add the chicken meat and flour, and fry for a further 5 minutes, stirring constantly.
4. Reduce heat and add the hot chicken stock, cook on low heat for 3 minutes.
5. Take off the heat and, while stirring constantly, add the whisked eggs.
6. Stir in the parsley, dill, lemon juice, nutmeg, salt and pepper.
7. With a little of the melted butter, grease a baking dish approximately 30 x 25 x 7 cm (12 x 10 x 3 in).
8. On the bottom and up the sides of the dish, place 6 sheets of filo pastry, each sheet generously brushed with melted butter before the next is placed.
9. Spoon the chicken mixture into this and fold the edges of the filo over the mixture.
10. Cover the mixture with the remaining 6 sheets of filo pastry, each in turn, as well as the top, well brushed with the melted butter.
11. Tuck the edges of the covering filo sheets around the inside edges of the baking dish.
12. Bake in the preheated oven for 30 minutes until golden. Serve hot.

Kota Pilári

Baked Chicken Pilaf
Serves 4

1 clove garlic, crushed
2 tablespoons tomato paste
2 tablespoons olive oil
1 teaspoon oregano
salt
freshly ground black pepper

8 chicken pieces, such as breasts, legs, thighs
1 cup (5 oz) long-grain rice
2½ cups (20 fl oz) boiling chicken stock (see p. 140) or water

1. Preheat the oven to 180°C (350°F/Gas 4).
2. Mix garlic, tomato paste, oil, oregano, salt and pepper.
3. Coat the chicken pieces with this mixture and place them in a deep baking dish or casserole.
4. Bake in preheated oven for 35 minutes, turn the pieces at least once.
5. Add the rice and stock or water.
6. Cover with lid or foil and cook for a further 30 minutes.
7. Take it out of the oven, let it stand for 10 minutes and serve with a green salad.

Kota Methismeni

Chicken with Brandy Cream Sauce
Serves 4

1.5 kg (3 lb) chicken, cut into serving pieces
¼ cup (2 fl oz) brandy
juice 1 lemon
salt

½ teaspoon white pepper
125 g (4 oz) butter
½ cup (4 fl oz) cream

1. Place the chicken pieces in a bowl, sprinkle with the brandy, lemon juice, salt and pepper and let them stand for 1 hour. Turn occasionally.
2. Heat the butter in a frying pan. Take the chicken pieces out of the bowl (save the brandy-lemon liquid), and sauté the pieces for about 10 to 15 minutes, until golden on all sides.
3. Reduce the heat and pour the brandy-lemon liquid over them. Simmer until almost all liquid has evaporated.
4. Add the cream, season to taste, and simmer for about 5 minutes. Serve with cooked peas or beans.

Right: The village of Makrinitsa on the slopes of Mt Pelion, high above the town of Volos.

Kota Kapamá

Braised Chicken in Tomato Sauce
Serves 4

8 chicken pieces, such as breast, legs, thighs
salt
freshly ground black pepper
60 g (2 oz) butter
1 onion, finely chopped
1 clove garlic, crushed

6 ripe tomatoes, peeled and chopped
2 tablespoons tomato paste
½ cup (4 fl oz) dry white wine
1 teaspoon powdered cinnamon
cooked hot pasta of your choice
grated Kefalotíri or Parmesan cheese

1. Preheat the oven to 150° C (300° F/Gas 2).
2. Sprinkle the chicken pieces with salt and pepper.
3. In a cast-iron casserole, fry the chicken pieces in butter until brown but not cooked. Set aside.
4. In the same casserole, sauté the onion and garlic until the onion is soft and transparent.
5. Add the tomatoes, tomato paste, wine and cinnamon. Season.
6. Return the chicken to the casserole. Cover and place in the preheated oven. Braise for 45 minutes.
7. Serve hot with pasta of your choice sprinkled with grated cheese.

Kotopoulo Avgolémono

Chicken with Egg-lemon Sauce
Serves 4

8 chicken pieces, such as breasts, legs, thighs
juice 2 lemons
1 teaspoon dried oregano
salt
freshly ground black pepper
60 g (2 oz) butter
1 cup (8 fl oz) dry white wine

1 cup (8 fl oz) chicken stock (see p. 140)
3 eggs, separated
1 tablespoon cornflour (cornstarch) [optional, if thicker sauce is required]
2 sprigs dill, chopped

1. Preheat the oven to 180°C (350°F/Gas 4).
2. Sprinkle the chicken pieces with lemon juice, oregano, salt, pepper and let stand for 2 hours.
3. In a casserole, heat the butter and fry the chicken pieces until light brown but not cooked.
4. Add wine and chicken stock. Cover, bring to the boil and braise in the oven for 1 hour.
5. Beat the egg whites with some salt until stiff.
6. Add the egg yolks and beat together.
7. Take the chicken pieces out of the casserole and arrange them on a serving platter.
8. Take out 1 cup (8 fl oz) of the cooking juice and mix it with the cornflour (optional).
9. Pour it back into the casserole and heat it until it thickens.
10. While beating constantly, add a cup of the thickened cooking juice to the egg mixture. Then, while continuing to beat vigorously, pour the egg mixture into the casserole.
11. Heat until it thickens but do not boil. Taste, and if necessary add more lemon juice, salt or pepper.
12. To serve, pour the sauce over the chicken pieces and serve sprinkled with the dill. Traditionally served with rice.

Kotopoulo Hilópittes apo ta Peloponnisa

Peloponnesian Chicken with Noodles
Serves 8-10

2 chickens, each weighing 1 kg (2 lb)
1½ teaspoons salt
freshly ground black pepper
90 g (3 oz) butter
2 large onions, chopped
1-2 cloves garlic, crushed (to taste)
1 cup (8 fl oz) dry white wine
6 ripe fresh tomatoes, peeled and chopped
1 cup (7 oz) tomato purée
2 stalks celery, finely chopped
3 sprigs parsley, chopped
¼ teaspoon cinnamon
500 g (1 lb) wide flat noodles
1 cup (4 oz) grated Kefalotíri or Parmesan cheese

1. Cut the chickens into serving pieces. Sprinkle them with salt and pepper and in a heavy frying pan sauté them in the butter until they are brown all over. Remove them from the pan and set them aside.
2. Sauté the onions and garlic in the butter until the onions are soft and transparent.
3. Return the chicken pieces, add the wine, cover and cook for 15 minutes.
4. Add tomatoes, tomato purée, celery, parsley and cinnamon. Cover the pot and simmer until the chicken pieces are tender.
5. Cook the noodles in salted water until done to your liking.
6. Take the chicken pieces out of the dish and arrange them in the centre of a large serving platter.
7. Put the noodles into the sauce and then place them around the chicken. Pour any remaining sauce over the chicken and noodles. Sprinkle with cheese and serve hot.

Right: Greek National Day, Corfu town.

Kapamá

Spicy Chicken
Serves 6

2 teaspoons salt
½ teaspoon freshly ground black pepper
½ teaspoon ground cloves
½ teaspoon ground cinnamon
juice 1 lemon
6 suprêmes of chicken (breast and lower part of wing)
90 g (3 oz) butter
1 onion, finely chopped

1 clove garlic, crushed
¾ cup (6 fl oz) water
½ cup (4 fl oz) dry white wine
3 tablespoons tomato paste
6 large tomatoes, peeled and chopped
1 teaspoon sugar
2 cups (10 oz) rice
½ cup (2 oz) grated Kefalotíri or Parmesan cheese (optional)

1. Combine salt, pepper, cloves, cinnamon and lemon juice and coat the chicken pieces with it.
2. In a large saucepan, melt the butter and lightly sauté the chicken pieces for about 5 minutes. Set aside and keep warm in a covered dish.
3. In the same saucepan, sauté the onion and garlic until onion is soft and transparent.
4. Add water, wine, tomato paste, tomatoes and sugar, and bring to the boil. Reduce heat, cover the saucepan and slowly cook for 1 hour. Season to taste.
5. Cook the rice to your liking.
6. To serve, put a portion of rice on each plate, place the chicken breast on top of the rice, pour the sauce over, and if desired sprinkle with cheese.

Kotopoulo Kokkinisto

Chicken Braised in White Wine
Serves 4

90 g (3 oz) butter
1.5 kg (3 lb) chicken, cut into 8 pieces
1 onion, chopped
1 clove garlic
4 tomatoes, peeled and chopped
1 tablespoon tomato paste

1 teaspoon dried oregano
½ teaspoon sugar
1 cup (8 fl oz) dry white wine
salt
freshly ground black pepper

1. Melt the butter and fry the chicken pieces until brown all round.
2. Add onion and garlic, and sauté until the onion is soft and transparent.
3. Add the rest of the ingredients, cover, and simmer over low heat for 1½ hours. Serve hot with a Greek salad.

Gallos Yemistós

Stuffed Roast Turkey
In Greece the most popular stuffing for turkey – which traditionally is served for Christmas and New Year – is rice. An unusual flavour is added by the use of feta cheese.

Serves 8-10

1 turkey 4-5 kg (8-10 lb), prebasted
juice 2 lemons
1 teaspoon grated lemon rind
salt
freshly ground black pepper

Stuffing:
2 onions, finely chopped
3 stalks celery, finely chopped
2 tablespoons oil
375 g (¾ lb) minced veal-pork mixture

turkey liver, chopped
2 cups (12 oz) cooked rice
1 cup (8 fl oz) red wine
½ cup (2 oz) pine nuts or chopped almonds
½ cup (2½ oz) currants
½ teaspoon nutmeg
1 teaspoon dried oregano
4 sprigs parsley, finely chopped
½ teaspoon cinnamon
125 g (4 oz) feta cheese, crumbled

1. Preheat the oven to 180° C (350° F/Gas 4).
2. Rub the cavity of the turkey with half of a mixture of lemon juice, lemon rind, salt and pepper. Let it stand while preparing the stuffing.
3. To make the stuffing, sauté the onions and celery in the oil.
4. Add the minced meat and the liver, and fry for 5 to 8 minutes.
5. Add the rice and wine, cook for 10 minutes.
6. Add the rest of the ingredients, mix well together, and if necessary adjust seasoning.
7. Stuff the mixture into the turkey body and neck cavities and secure the openings with skewers.
8. Rub the skin with the rest of the seasoned lemon juice. Cover it with foil.
9. Place the turkey in the preheated oven and roast for 2½ hours with the foil. Remove the foil and continue cooking so as to brown the skin, for 1 more hour or until done.
10. When cooked, remove it from the oven and let it stand for 10 to 15 minutes before carving.
11. Arrange the carved pieces in the middle of a serving platter and place the stuffing around it. Do not worry if some parts of the turkey are undercooked. After carving, and while preparing a gravy from the cooking juices, put the platter in the turned-off oven to keep warm. The underdone parts will set during that time. An overcooked turkey would be dry and tasteless.

PASTRIES AND DESSERTS

In Greece people frequently have fruit after a meal, and if desserts are eaten, they are served at least an hour after dinner.

Greeks enjoy sweets and often have them with their coffee. The number of shops selling pastry gives an indication of how fond Greeks are of sweets. Everywhere you turn there is a tempting display of delicious syrupy cakes, colourful glazed fruit and pastries of many kinds. Greeks will have them anytime of the day. In coffee shops and at tables along the pavements, they sit, sip many cups of coffee and nibble at nutty, honey-drenched pastries.

They are leisurely eaters, so there is no great hurry. They sit around and let the meal settle down. An hour or so later they indulge in the favourite part of the meal: the dessert.

Most Greek pastries and sweets are part of Middle Eastern tradition which favours combinations of nuts, especially walnuts and pistachios, with honey and fruit such as figs ånd dates. The use of filo pastry is extensive.

One of the results is the famous Baklavá, layers of paper-thin pastry sheets, ground nuts soaked with a honey syrup, and sprinkled with pistachios. Who can resist the inviting and appetising trays of this typically diamond-shaped pastry?

Many varieties of halva are displayed and the rosewater-scented Loukoumia (also known as Turkish delight), its many colours barely discernible under the generous dusting of icing sugar.

Rich yellow custard oozes out of custard rolls. Pyramids of various biscuits, most of them sprinkled with some kind of nuts, are piled high in the shop windows.

Greeks must be among the highest sugar consumers, for not only do they unashamedly enjoy all these sweets, but they also take lots of sugar in their strong and aromatic Greek coffee. Maybe the inevitable glass of water that traditionally is drunk with the coffee makes all the difference.

Pileas Restaurant, Hania, Mt Pelion

The Pileas serves hearty local dishes which, especially in winter, is the right type of food after a day's skiing on the nearby mountain.

The Fassouláda, a dried white bean soup prepared with onions, carrots and tomatoes, is almost a meal itself.

Galotini, a dish of feta cheese soaked in milk or yogurt, is served with all meals.

The best-known dish of the region is Spengiofai, a spicy pork sausage served with green peppers, tomatoes and small onions – a thirst-inducing combination with which the host serves Kokkinéli, a robust red wine.

Not far from Hania and slightly lower is Makrenitsa, a picturesque village which, because of its crisp fresh air even in the midst of summer, has always been a popular retreat from the heat of the lowlands. In recent times, the Greek Tourist Organisation has been converting old mansions into guesthouses, and a holiday in Makrenitsa is quite an experience. There is only pedestrian traffic allowed into the village and the mule is the only means of transport.

Right foreground: Dried White Bean Soup (p. 30); Sausages with green peppers, onions and tomatoes (p. 96); Greek Feta with yogurt.

Tsouréki

Plaited Sweet Almond Bread
Makes 2 loaves

1 packet active dry yeast
½ cup (4 fl oz) lukewarm water
½ cup (4 fl oz) water
1 tablespoon Ouzo
½ teaspoon ground cinnamon
½ teaspoon aniseed
½ teaspoon grated orange peel
½ cup (4 fl oz) milk

125 g (4 oz) butter
200 g (6½ oz) sugar
¼ teaspoon salt
750g (1½ lb) flour
1 egg, lightly beaten in
  2 tablespoons water
60 g (2 oz) slivered almonds

1. Dissolve yeast in the lukewarm water and leave to activate for 20 minutes.
2. In a saucepan, bring to the boil the water, Ouzo, cinnamon, aniseed, orange peel, milk, butter, sugar and salt. Stir until sugar dissolves, and cool.
3. Add the yeast to this mixture.
4. Place the flour in a large mixing bowl and stir the liquid into the flour until dough leaves the sides of the bowl easily. If necessary, adjust consistency by adding more flour or more water.
5. On a floured surface, knead the dough for about 10 minutes until it is smooth and elastic.
6. Grease the bowl and return the dough to it. Cover with a teatowel and stand it in a warm draught-free place to rise until double, approximately 2 hours.
7. Punch down the dough and knead lightly.
8. Divide the dough into two parts and each, in turn, into three. Roll out each into a strand 35 cm (14 in) long. Plait three strands together and, using some water, press the ends together. Plait the other three strands to make the second loaf.
9. Place the two loaves on a greased baking dish 5 cm (2 in) apart, cover with teatowel and permit to rise for a further 2 hours.
10. Preheat the oven to 180℃ (350°F/Gas 4).
11. Brush the loaves with the egg-water mixture and sprinkle the tops with the almonds.
12. In the bottom of the oven, place a bowl with boiling water; this will help to produce a crisp crust.
13. Bake for 45 minutes until brown and the loaves sound hollow when tapped.
14. Cool on wire rack.

Melópitta

Spicy Apple Pie
Baked in a dish 25 cm (10 in) square

Serves 12

Pastry:
2 cups (8 oz) flour
45 g (1½ oz) sugar
½ teaspoon salt
1 teaspoon baking powder
60 g (2 oz) butter
2 tablespoons vegetable oil
½ cup (4 fl oz) water

Filling:
6 apples (Granny Smith), peeled,
   cored and roughly diced,
   sprinkled with lemon juice to
   prevent discolouring
1 cup (5 oz) brown sugar
1½ teaspoons cinnamon
½ teaspoon nutmeg
¼ teaspoon ground cloves
1 egg, lightly beaten
honey and yogurt for garnish

1. Preheat the oven to 200°C (400°F/Gas 6).
2. To make the pastry, in a large mixing bowl combine the flour, sugar, salt and baking powder.
3. Using your hands and working rapidly, mix in the butter. Stir in the oil and water. Knead lightly for 1 minute. Divide the pastry into two.
4. On a floured surface roll out two 25 cm (10 in) squares. Place one on the bottom of the dish and place the other between plastic film. Refrigerate both.
5. To make the filling, combine all the ingredients and spread them in the pastry-lined dish.
6. Cover the filling with the remaining pastry. Brush the top with the beaten egg.
7. Bake in the preheated oven for 45 minutes until golden brown. Cool on wire rack.
8. To serve, cut into squares and top each slice with honey and some yogurt.

Baklavá

Yields 30 pieces in a 33 x 23 x 5 cm (13 x 9 x 2 in) baking tin

1 cup (8 oz) melted unsalted
  butter
500 g (1 lb) walnuts, finely
  chopped
250 g (8 oz) almonds, blanched
  and finely chopped
¼ cup (2 oz) sugar
2 teaspoons cinnamon
¼ teaspoon ground cloves
500 g (1 lb) filo pastry

Syrup:
220 g (7 oz) sugar
1 cup (12 oz) honey
2 cups (16 fl oz) water
juice 1 lemon
2 whole cloves
1 sliver of lemon rind

1. Preheat the oven to 160° C (325° F/Gas 3).
2. With a little of the melted butter, brush the inside of the baking tin.
3. In a bowl, mix well together the nuts, sugar, cinnamon and cloves.
4. Over the bottom of the tin, place 10 sheets of filo pastry, each sheet generously brushed with butter before the next is placed. Sprinkle the top sheet with some of the nut-sugar mixture.
5. Place 2 buttered sheets of filo pastry on top and sprinkle with the nut mixture. Repeat this process until all the nut mixture is used up. There should be 15-20 layers.
6. Trim along the edges and brush the top with the remaining butter.
7. Score the top layer diagonally with parallel lines.
8. Place in the preheated oven and bake for 30 minutes.
9. Move up to the top of the oven for a further 30 minutes. If the top browns too quickly, cover with aluminium foil.
10. While the baklavá is baking, prepare the syrup. Combine all ingredients, heat and stir to dissolve sugar.
11. Bring to the boil and boil briskly for 10 minutes.
12. Strain, cool, and pour half of the syrup over the hot baklavá.
13. Let it stand for 30 minutes, then pour over the remainder of the syrup.
14. Leave overnight before cutting.

Right: Flock of sheep, Volos.

Ghalatoboureko

Custard Semolina Pie
Makes a pie 30 x 23 x 5 cm (12 x 9 x 2 in)

6 eggs
185 g (6 oz) sugar
1½ cups (8 oz) semolina
7 cups (1.75 litres) milk
1 teaspoon grated lemon peel
60 g (2 oz) butter

¾ cup (6 oz) melted butter
16 filo pastry sheets

Syrup:
500 g (1 lb) sugar
1 cup (8 fl oz) water
juice 1 lemon

1. Preheat the oven to 180° C (350° F/Gas 4).
2. Cream the eggs and sugar together until thick.
3. Add semolina, milk and lemon peel.
4. Cook over low heat, stirring continuously until the mixture thickens.
5. Remove from heat and stir in 60 g butter.
6. With some of the melted butter, brush the inside of the baking tin.
7. On the bottom and up the sides of the dish, place 8 sheets of filo pastry, each sheet generously brushed with melted butter before the next is placed.
8. Spoon the mixture into this and fold the edges of the filo pastry over at the top.
9. Cover the mixture with the remaining 8 sheets of filo pastry, each in turn, as well as the top, well brushed with melted butter.
10. Tuck the edges of the covering filo sheets around the inside edges of the pan.
11. With a sharp knife, cut through the top 3 sheets in parallel lines forming 7.5 cm (3 in) squares.
12. Bake in the preheated oven for 45 minutes. Allow to cool.
13. To prepare the syrup, combine all the ingredients, heat, and stir to dissolve sugar.
14. Bring to boil and boil for 5 to 8 minutes.
15. Cool and pour lukewarm syrup over the pie.
16. Serve cold, cut into squares.

Amigthalotá

Almond 'Pears'

This recipe originates from the island of Hydra.

500 g (1 lb) ground almond meal, available in nut speciality shops (if not, whole blanched nuts may be ground in a food processor or blender)

1 cup (8 oz) sugar

75 g (2½ oz) semolina

1½ cups (12 fl oz) orange flower water

1 cup (6 oz) icing (confectioners') sugar

cloves

1. Preheat the oven to 200°C (400° F/Gas 6).
2. Mix the ground almonds and 2 tablespoons of the sugar in a mortar and grind them finely. A food processor is very handy for this purpose, in which case using 1 cupful of almond meal and some of the sugar at a time, process until the mixture is very fine.
3. Add semolina, and some orange flower water. The texture of the mixture should be such as to keep its shape when formed into pear-shaped balls. If necessary, add more orange flower water or more semolina.
4. Form the mixture into walnut-sized 'pears' and insert a clove to form the 'stalk'.
5. Arrange 'pears' on a buttered and floured baking tray and bake in the preheated oven for 20 minutes.
6. Cool, dip them into orange flower water and sprinkle them with icing sugar. Before serving, coat them with icing sugar again.

Halvás

Halva
Serves 6

1 cup (8 fl oz) milk
1 cup (8 fl oz) water
1 cup (8 oz) sugar
1½ teaspoons vanilla extract
125 g (4 oz) unsalted butter

½ cup (2 oz) pine nuts or
   unsalted pistachios
1 cup (5 oz) coarse semolina
1 teaspoon cinnamon

1. Gently boil milk, water and sugar for 15 minutes, add vanilla extract and take off the heat.
2. Melt the butter in a frying pan and lightly sauté the nuts.
3. Add semolina to the frying pan and cook over low heat for 15 minutes. Do not allow to become too brown.
4. Take off the heat and slowly add the milk mixture. Be careful, as it may spatter.
5. Simmer over low heat for 5 minutes or until mixture is very thick and comes away from sides of pan.
6. Spread the mixture about 2.5-4 cm (1-1½ in) thick in a buttered dish. Allow to cool, about 1½ hours.
7. To serve, unmould on to a decorative plate, cut into small squares and sprinkle with cinnamon.

Right: Exterior Arvanitia Beach Restaurant, Nafplio.

Loukoumathes

Fritters with Honey Syrup
Makes 36 fritters

Syrup:
1 cup (8 oz) sugar
½ cup (6 oz) honey
½ cup (4 fl oz) water
juice 1 lemon

Fritters:
1 tablespoon dried yeast
1¼ cups (10 fl oz) lukewarm water
3 cups (12 oz) flour
½ teaspoon salt
½ cup (4 fl oz) lukewarm milk
1 egg
oil for frying
1 tablespoon cinnamon

1. To make the syrup, combine the ingredients in a saucepan and, while stirring constantly, cook until the syrup thickens sufficiently to coat a spoon.
2. Pour the hot syrup into a heatproof container (a jug would be best) and set aside.
3. To make the fritters, mix the yeast with 3-4 tablespoons of the lukewarm water and let it stand to rise until the mixture doubles in volume.
4. Put the flour and salt in a large mixing bowl.
5. In a separate bowl, mix the yeast, the rest of the lukewarm water, the milk and egg together. Gradually incorporate it into the flour, then beat vigorously until the dough is smooth and just firm enough to hold its shape. If necessary, adjust its consistency by adding either more lukewarm water or more flour.
6. Cover the bowl with a teatowel and stand it in a warm draught-free place for about 45 minutes to 1 hour until the dough doubles in volume.
7. Preheat 8-10 cm (3-4 in) of oil in a saucepan.
8. Dip a tablespoon in cold water and pick up a level spoonful of the dough and push it with another spoon into the hot oil. Do up to 6 fritters at a time. Fry for 2 to 3 minutes until golden brown.
9. Keep them warm in a preheated oven.
10. To serve, heap the fritters on a serving dish, pour the syrup over them and sprinkle with cinnamon. The syrup may be served separately.

Kourambiéthes

Walnut Butter Biscuits
Makes about 24 biscuits

250 g (8 oz) butter, melted and
  cooled
½ cup (3 oz) icing
  (confectioners') sugar
1 teaspoon baking powder

2 cups (8 oz) flour
¼ cup (1 oz) finely chopped
  walnuts

1. Preheat the oven to 180° C (350° F/Gas 4).
2. Mix the butter, 30 g (1 oz) of the sugar and the baking powder in a large
   mixing bowl. Then gradually add the flour, beating constantly. Finally
   add the walnuts.
3. With floured hand, form 1½ tablespoons of the dough into round
   biscuit shapes, 4 cm (1½ in) in diameter and 1.5 cm (½ in) thick. Place
   them on a floured baking tray, keeping them 2.5 cm (1 in) apart.
4. Bake them for about 15 minutes until they are light, brown and firm.
5. Cool them on a cake rack and sprinkle them with the remainder of the
   icing sugar.

Tiganites

Fritter Puffs
Makes about 36 puffs

1 cup (8 fl oz) water
125 g (4 oz) butter
1 teaspoon sugar
1 cup (4 oz) self-raising flour

4 eggs
2 tablespoons rum or brandy
oil for frying
½ cup (3 oz) icing
  (confectioners') sugar

1. Put the water, butter and sugar in a saucepan and heat it until the butter
   has melted.
2. Stir in the flour and cook while stirring vigorously until the mixture
   leaves the sides.
3. Take the saucepan off the heat and beat in the eggs one at a time, also
   add the rum or brandy. If you have an electric mixer, put the mixture
   into the mixing bowl and beat at high speed while adding the eggs.
4. Heat the oil in a saucepan or deep frying pan until very hot.
5. With a wet teaspoon, take some batter and push it off with another
   teaspoon into the oil.
6. Cook until the puffs are light brown.
7. When cooked, pile them up on a serving dish and dust them with icing
   sugar. Serve lukewarm.

Thiples

Deep-fried sweet pastry
Makes about 50

3 eggs, separated, at room
    temperature
1 teaspoon baking powder
juice ½ orange
¼ cup (2 fl oz) vegetable oil
2 cups (8 oz) flour

4 cups (1 litre) oil for frying
2 cups (1 lb 4 oz) honey
1 cup (8 fl oz) water
1½ cups (6 oz) finely chopped
    walnuts or almonds
cinnamon for sprinkling

1. Whip the egg whites with the baking powder until they hold their peaks.
2. Beat the egg yolks and mix them with the egg whites.
3. Add orange juice, oil and flour, mix well, and transfer to a lightly floured board. Knead for 15 minutes. The dough will be sticky.
4. Divide it into 6 or 8 parts. Wrap in plastic film and refrigerate for 1 to 2 hours.
5. Take out one ball at a time and roll it out paper-thin on a floured board.
6. With a sharp knife, cut into rectangles 7.5 cm (3 in) long and 5 cm (2 in) wide. Fold them into triangles.
7. Heat the frying oil until very hot, drop the Thiples, one at a time, into the oil and fry for about 1 minute until golden brown. Keep oil free of crumbs.
8. Carefully remove with slotted spoon on to some paper towelling.
9. Stack them between layers of paper towels.
10. Boil the honey and water for 5 minutes and set aside.
11. Place the Thiples in layers on a serving plate, pour some honey over each and sprinkle with nuts and cinnamon.
12. Carefully spoon the Thiples on to individual serving plates and spoon any excess syrup on to them.

Right: One of the many holy Monasteries on Mt Athos.

Ravani

Greek Sugar Cake
20 servings

3 cups (24 fl oz) water
2¾ cups (1 lb 6 oz) sugar
juice ½ lemon
250 g (8 oz) unsalted butter
5 eggs, beaten
2 teaspoons vanilla essence

2 cups (8 oz) self-raising flour
1 cup (5 oz) semolina
3 teaspoons baking powder
½ cup (4 fl oz) cream, whipped
¼ cup (1 oz) chopped walnuts or
   almonds

1. Preheat the oven to 180°C (350°F/Gas 4).
2. To make a syrup, over medium heat boil the water, 2 cups (16 oz) of the sugar and the lemon juice for 15 minutes. Set aside to cool.
3. Melt the butter, pour it into a bowl and add remaining ¾ cup of sugar. Stir until sugar is dissolved, beat in the eggs and add the vanilla essence.
4. Mix the flour, semolina and baking powder in a bowl and then stir it well into the sugar-egg mixture.
5. Grease a baking tin about 36 x 25 x 5 cm (14 x 10 x 2 in). Pour in the mixture and smooth the top.
6. Bake in the preheated oven for 30 to 35 minutes until medium brown.
7. While still in the tin, cut the cake into squares or diamond shapes.
8. Pour some syrup over the hot cake. When absorbed, pour over some more. Repeat until all syrup is used.
9. Serve at room temperature garnished with whipped cream and nuts.

Melomakarona

Honey Shortbread
Makes 24-30

3 cups (12 oz) flour
1 teaspoon baking powder
1 teaspoon bicarbonate of soda
  (baking soda)
1 cup (8 fl oz) olive oil
¼ cup (2 oz) sugar
½ cup (4 fl oz) brandy
¼ cup (2 fl oz) orange juice

1 tablespoon grated orange rind
½ cup (2 oz) chopped walnuts
1 teaspoon cinnamon

Syrup:
1 cup (10 oz) honey
½ cup (4 oz) sugar
1 cup (8 fl oz) water

1. Preheat the oven to 180°C (350°F/Gas 4).
2. In a bowl, combine flour, baking powder and bicarbonate of soda. Mix well together.
3. Combine oil, sugar, brandy, orange juice and orange rind and gradually incorporate it into the flour. The dough should be easy to knead.
4. Knead it lightly.
5. Roll it out and cut round or oval shapes about 6-8 cm (2½-3 in).
6. Place them on a greased baking tray and bake in the preheated oven for 20 minutes, until light brown.
7. To make the syrup, mix the honey, sugar and water and boil for 5 minutes. Allow to cool.
8. Dip the shortbread in the syrup, place them on a serving plate and sprinkle with chopped walnuts and cinnamon.

Karithópitta

Nut Cake
Use a 34 x 23 x 5 cm (13 x 9 x 2 in) baking tin.

Makes 36 pieces

Cake:
250 g (8 oz) softened butter
2 cups (14 oz) sugar
2 teaspoons vanilla essence
8 eggs
1 teaspoon baking powder
½ teaspoon bicarbonate of soda (baking soda)
2 teaspoons cinnamon
1 cup (4 oz) cornmeal (polenta)
1 cup (4 oz) flour

½ cup (4 fl oz) milk
2 cups (8 oz) coarsely chopped walnuts, hazelnuts or almonds

Syrup:
3 cups (24 fl oz) water
1 cup (7 oz) sugar
1 cup (10 oz) honey
½ stick cinnamon
1 orange slice with peel
1 teaspoon lemon juice

1. Preheat the oven to 190°C (375°F/Gas 5).
2. Cream the butter and 2 cups of sugar until the sugar is dissolved.
3. Add vanilla essence and eggs, beat for 2 minutes. Add baking powder, bicarbonate of soda and cinnamon, beat for further 2 minutes.
4. Mix in cornmeal (polenta), flour, milk and nuts.
5. Pour the mixture into the greased baking tin and bake in the preheated oven for 40 minutes.
6. To make the syrup, combine the ingredients in a saucepan. While stirring, bring it to the boil and simmer over low heat for 40 minutes.
7. Remove cinnamon stick and orange slice.
8. Take the cake out of the oven, remove it from the tin and put into a deep dish. Slowly pour the syrup over the cake, permitting syrup to be absorbed. Cool and cut into square pieces. Let it stand for 4 to 6 hours or overnight before serving.

Rizógalo

Rice Pudding
Serves 4

⅓ cup (2½ fl oz) water
⅓ cup (2 oz) long-grain rice
4 cups (1 litre) milk
¾ cup (6 oz) sugar

60 g (2 oz) butter
2 eggs, well beaten
1 teaspoon vanilla essence
½ teaspoon cinnamon

1. Boil the water, add rice, cover and over low heat cook rice for 5 minutes until water is absorbed. Remove from heat and keep covered.
2. In another saucepan, bring the milk to the boil and stir in the rice and cook over low heat for about 35 minutes, stirring occasionally so that rice does not stick.
3. Gently mix in the sugar until it is dissolved. Take off the heat and stir in the butter. Cool to room temperature.
4. Stir 1 cup of the cooled rice into the eggs, return it to the saucepan, heat and stir over low heat for about 15 minutes. Rice should be light yellow and creamy. Add vanilla and take off heat.
5. Pour the rice into a large serving dish or individual serving bowls. Refrigerate and serve sprinkled with cinnamon.

BASIC RECIPES

Chicken Stock

Makes 10 cups (2.5 litres)

1.5 kg (3 lb) boiling chicken with giblets
8-12 cups (2-3 litres) water
2 carrots, sliced
1 turnip, sliced
3 stalks celery, sliced

2 onions, unpeeled and halved
½ bunch parsley, roughly chopped
1 sprig thyme, chopped
6 peppercorns
3 bay leaves

1. In a large saucepan combine all the ingredients, making certain that the heart, stomach and liver have been properly cleaned.
2. Bring slowly to the boil and continue to simmer over low heat for 2 to 2½ hours.
3. Let all the ingredients cool in the stock, then strain, refrigerate and degrease it.
4. Discard the vegetables but keep the chicken. Remove the meat from the bones. It can be either chopped and used in a chicken soup or minced and made into chicken croquettes.
5. Use the stock in the preparation of soups and sauces. It may be refrigerated and will keep for 3 to 4 days or frozen when it may be kept for months.

Psarózoumo

Basic Fish Stock
Serves 6-8

1.5-2 kg (3-4 lb) fresh fish heads, bones and tails, prawn or crayfish shells
8-12 cups (2-3 litres) cold water
1 cup (8 fl oz) dry white wine
6 peppercorns
2 large onions, chopped

2 stalks celery, chopped
3 bay leaves
1 tablespoon oregano
3 sprigs parsley, chopped
salt (optional)

1. Place all the fish parts and shells in a large pot and add all the other ingredients.
2. Very slowly bring the water to the boil, then turn down the heat to low, and simmer slowly for 45 minutes.
3. Let it cool. When cold, strain the stock through a sieve or colander.
4. Season and eat it as a soup. Or unseasoned, use it in the preparation of other soups or sauces. Can be refrigerated or frozen when it will keep for weeks.

Vouthinos Zoumos

Home-made Beef Stock
Makes 6-8 cups (1.5-2 litres)

2-3 tablespoons olive oil
2 kg (4 lb) pig's trotters, shin
    bone, veal knuckles, or similar
1 kg (2 lb) shin beef, cut into
    cubes
3 stalks celery, chopped
    (including leaves)
2 carrots, sliced

3 onions, quartered
6 peppercorns
3 bay leaves
1 clove
12 cups (3 litres) cold water

1. Preheat the oven to 200°C (400° F/Gas 6).
2. Pour the oil into a heavy roasting dish.
3. Place the bones, meat, celery, carrots and onions into the dish and roast
   for about 30 minutes, turning all ingredients occasionally.
4. Transfer everything to a large pot and add the rest of the ingredients.
5. Bring slowly to the boil and simmer gently over low heat for 4 to 5 hours.
   Skim off any foam rising to the surface.
6. Strain the stock through a fine sieve, save the meat for later use, and
   discard bones and vegetables.
7. If the stock is not required immediately for use in soups or sauces,
   refrigerate or freeze, and discard any fat that may have set on the
   surface.

Mayonnaise

Makes 1 ½ cups

2 egg yolks
1¼ cups (10 fl oz) olive oil
1 tablespoon French mustard

juice of 1 lemon
salt
freshly ground black pepper

1. Place the egg yolks and mustard into a bowl and beat with a wire whisk
   until well blended.
2. Add the oil, drop by drop at first, then in a thin stream as the
   mayonnaise thickens.
3. Add the lemon juice, salt and pepper.

INDEX